Tastes & Tales

of the

Great Pine Level

For the benefit of the Jay Historical Society

Volume 1

Appreciation

We appreciate all of your submissions to the *Tastes & Tales of the Great Pine Level, Volume 1.* Please accept our apologies for any omissions or errors. The proceeds of this cookbook, sponsored and compiled by members of the Jay Historical Society, will help support the Jay Museum. Thank you for your continuing support.

Dedication

This first volume of *Tastes and Tales of the Great Pine Level* is dedicated to those who came before us. Perhaps not many of them learned to preheat their ovens to 350 degrees. Instead, they may have stirred a pot over an open fire or stoked big wood-burning stoves to warm, hot, or hotter. Still, they cooked good food--simple maybe, but undeniably satisfying. Perhaps what they cooked tomorrow often depended upon what was leftover today. Maybe today's leftover biscuits showed up in tomorrow's bread pudding. It is not unlikely that today's leftover peas and creamed corn were added to a quart of canned tomatoes and served as tomorrow's vegetable soup.

Ah, but who wouldn't declare one's very own mother or grandmother or great-grandmother made the *very* tastiest of biscuits or pies or soups? If your relative's best recipes are not included in *Tastes and Tales of the Great Pine Level, Volume I*, then send them in for *Volume II*. We will print their pictures and stories and recipes. Allow to preserve your memorable meals for generations yet unborn.

Layout and Cover Design by Teresa Scott Hendricks

Tastes & Tales
of the
Great Pine Level

Introduction

These recipes, along with the accompanying photographs and stories, each reveal a bit of our collective heritage. For the most part, our northwest Florida folks cooked plain food. Plain means good; it means nothing has to be poured on top to disguise the real taste. Plain can also mean surprising: What about a pound cake recipe which calls for eight eggs—and no other liquids? (It has been tried recently, and it's *still* good!) You will discover this and many other delightful surprises in ***Tastes and Tales of the Great Pine Level, Volume I.***

To be completely authentic, we would have had to include those always handy measurements called a "dash," a "dab," and a "pinch." In this instance, though, we decided our readers would prefer usefulness over authenticity.

May you relish this collection of memories which speak the language of food!

Tastes & Tales
of the
Great Pine Level

TABLE OF CONTENTS

Appetizers & Beverages	5
Soups & Salads	17
Biscuits & Bread	25
Vegetables & Side Dishes	37
Meat & Game	61
Fish & Seafood	81
Poultry	93
Cakes & Cookies	107
Pies, Desserts, & Candy	157
Other	187

Appetizers & Beverages
of the
Great Pine Level

Ann Cannon's Punch

2 46 oz. cans pineapple juice
1 ginger ale (small)
1 tsp. almond flavoring (or to taste)
1 cup sugar

Mix pineapple, sugar, and almond flavoring, chill. Add ginger ale just prior to serving. Makes 1 gallon.

Submitted by: Jane Hayes

Hanky Pankies

1 lb. sausage
1 lbs. ground beef
1 loaf of pantry rye (small party bread)
1 lb. Velveeta cheese
1 tsp. oregano

In skillet, brown sausage, ground beef and oregano; drain well. Add cheese; melt with sausage and ground beef mixture. Spoon out on rye bread. Place on lightly greased cookie sheet. Heat in 350 degree oven until cheese mixture has melted. You can freeze this on a cookie sheet as well then reheat.

Submitted by: Miriam Hudgens Ingram

Mary Evelyn's Cream Cheese Crescent Rolls

2 cans crescent rolls
1 1/2 cups sugar
2 8 oz. pkgs. cream cheese
1 stick of butter melted

Butter 8 x 13 dish. Layer one can of crescent rolls in bottom of dish. Mix cream cheese, and sugar and pour over crescent rolls. Unroll the other can of rolls and put on top of cheese mixture. Pour butter on top, and sprinkle a little sugar over.
Bake at 350 degrees for 30 minutes.

Submitted by: Mary Evelyn Hoomes Hendricks

Mary Frances' Banana Chunks

This recipe has been a staple and much coveted treat at Mt Carmel Methodist Church for showers and receptions.

35 banana chunks
1 1/2 cups of sour cream
2 1/2 - 3 cups of coconut, sweetened & shredded
3 cups of whipped topping

Mix whipped topping and sour cream. Place coconut in separate container. Dip banana chunks in whipped topping mixture, and then cover with coconut. Chill overnight

Submitted by: Mary Frances Hayes Hendricks

Pineapple Cheese Ball

2 8oz. Pkgs. cream cheese
2 Tbsp. onion, chopped
1/4 tsp. salt
2 cups pecans, chopped
1/4 cup green pepper, chopped
1- small can crushed pineapple, drained

Beat cream cheese with fork until smooth. Gradually add pineapple, onion, pepper, salt. Add 1 cup of pecans. Mix well, shape in to ball. Roll in remaining pecans until covered. Chill overnight

Submitted by: Glenda Henderson Hayes

Susie Bush's Crescent Roll Delight

2 cans of crescent rolls
1 8 oz. pkg. of cream cheese
1 can green chiles
1 pkg. ground sausage, browned & drained

Layer one can of crescent rolls in bottom of lightly greased 9 x 13 pan. When sausage is cooked then drained, mix green chiles, and cream cheese with sausage. Gently spread over crescent rolls, then top with remaining crescent rolls. Bake at 350 degrees until crescent rolls have browned, about 15 –20 minutes.

Submitted by: Jane Hayes

Ann Cannon's Meatballs

Florence Ann Bell Cannon

1 lg. bag meatballs, frozen
1 jar chili sauce
1 can cranberry sauce

Mix chili and cranberry sauce and heat. Get ice off of meatballs, place on cookie sheet and bake until water is out. (about 20 minutes)
Mix meatballs and sauce, keep warm in a crock-pot or chafing dish.
If cooking a large bag of meatballs, triple recipe, and it will serve about 200 people.

Granny's Green Punch

Lola Blackmon

This punch recipe was a favorite of all the grandchildren and children of Lola Blackmon. Granny made this punch for us every Easter which we all enjoyed after our egg hunts. It is still a favorite today and we always think of Granny when we have it.

1 pkg. lemon lime kool-aide
1 lg. can pineapple juice
1 3/4 cup sugar

In a 2 quart container pour in sugar and pkg. of kool-aide. Add water until container is half full. Stir until sugar is dissolved. Add can of pineapple juice, stir, add water to fill container.

Submitted by: Sheila Cobb Hendricks, granddaughter

Judy & Kayla's Breakfast Casserole

Every Christmas Eve, we make this and pop it in the oven on Christmas morning for a great hassle free breakfast.

1 lb. sausage, browned & drained
6 slices of bread (remove crusts)
8 eggs, beaten
2 cups grated cheddar cheese
2 cups milk
1 tsp. salt

Spoon prepared sausage in to bottom of 9 x13 baking dish. Combine beaten eggs, milk, and salt. Tear bread into small pieces and add to egg mixture, along with grated cheese. Pour onto sausage. Refrigerate over night. Bake 45 minutes at 350 degrees. May be frozen and reheated with foil covering.

Submitted by: Judy and Kayla Flowers, mother & daughter

Lona's Famous Sweet Tea

Miles and Lona Harrison

Miles and Lona Harrison operated Circle Drive Cafe located on the corner of Hwy 89 and Hwy 4 in the 1960's. They rented the building form Arthur Lee & Valentine Day for $25 per month. In late 1969, they rented a building on Commerce Street from J.F. Shell for $50 per month. They moved from the Circle Drive to Commerce Street and named their new business The City Cafe. Lona served home-cooked, made- from-scratch meals.

The City Cafe opened at 5:00 a.m. which required Lona and Miles to be there much earlier to make preparations to open. I can remember Tim McCurdy, who became like a family member to us, always being the first customer of the day. He had breakfast every morning at The City Cafe before heading to work at Monsanto. Other regulars were J.T. Jones, Wiley McCurdy and Hagood Carden.

In 1970, the Discovery Oil Well was drilled and things really got crazy. There was not near enough room for all who wanted to eat at the cafe. So Lona and Miles rented the building adjacent to them and cut a doorway between them. This is when they started serving cafeteria style meals, to accommodate all the diners. One of the community favorites was Lona's famous sweet tea. It was great!

The City Cafe became the favorite eatery of the oil field personnel. To find anyone connected to the oil industry, one only needed to go to the cafe and ask Lona if they had been in for lunch.

7 individual tea bags
1 quart of water   4 cups
pinch of soda
2 cups sugar

Put tea bags, soda and water in boiler. Bring just to a boil. Remove from heat, cover and let set about 30 minutes.

Put 2 cups of sugar in 1 gallon pitcher. Pour water from steeped tea in pitcher and stir. Continue adding water on tea bags and pouring in pitcher, until water is clear. Fill gallon pitcher completely full of water, stir and serve.

Submitted by: Evelyn Jordan, daughter

Meaty Cheese Dip

Jay UMC Children and Youth, circa 1981

This recipe has always been a hit at parties and church functions.

1 lb. ground beef, browned
2 lbs. Velveeta , cut in 1 inch cubes
1 clove garlic, minced
1 (10 oz.) can tomatoes & green chiles
2 Tbsp. Chile seasoning mix

Cook ground beef and garlic until meat is well browned, stirring to crumble meat. Remove from heat, drain well and set aside.
Place cheese, tomatoes, and green chiles in top of double boiler, bring water to boil, reduce heat to low, cook until cheese is melted stirring constantly. Stir in ground beef and chili seasoning mix. Serve warm with corn chips and assorted crackers.
Note: can utilize microwave instead of stovetop to melt cheese mixture.

Smoked Ham Balls

Glenda Burkhead came from a family of ten children and learned early on how to cook. Her father owned and operated a cotton gin in Jay for many years. When she grew up, she went to work in Washington, D.C. ,for the FBI under J. Edgar Hoover. When she retired, she moved back to Jay and became an active member of the community.

1 1/2 cups brown sugar	1/4 tsp. salt
1/2 cup vinegar	1 1/2 lbs. ground pork
1/2 cup water	1 lb. ground smoked ham
1 tsp. dry mustard	2 cups bread crumbs
2 eggs, well beaten	1 cup sweet milk

Combine brown sugar, vinegar, water, and mustard. Stir until sugar is dissolved. Combine meats, crumbs, eggs, salt, and milk; mix well. Form in two small balls. Place in casserole. Pour brown sugar mixture over meatballs. Bake in slow oven at 275 degrees for 1 1/4 hours. Baste frequently with sauce.

Smoked Oyster Roll

In the 1970's, the oil boom hit Jay, and it was bustling again. Many people went to work in the oil industry and people from many different areas of the country once again migrated here. This recipe was given to Glenda Hayes by Doris Bostic. Doris was the wife of Roy Bostic who worked with Ralph Hayes, Sr. at Amerada Hess.

3 oz. can smoked oysters,	1/8 tsp. salt
8 oz. cream cheese, softened	1/2 tsp. garlic powder
2 Tbsp. Mayonnaise	1/2 cup nuts, chopped

Drain Oysters; chop fine and set aside. Combine next 4 ingredients. Spread cheese mixture about 1/8" thick in 8 x10 rectangle on a sheet of wax paper. Combine nuts and oysters, mix well, and then sprinkle evenly over cheese mixture. Roll up jellyroll fashion, picking off wax paper as you go. Sprinkle chives evenly over a clean sheet of wax paper and roll until cheese is completely coated. Wrap in wax paper and chill overnight or until firm. Serve with crackers.

Soups & Salads
of the
Great Pine Level

Dorothy Mitchell Scott

This potato salad was my mother's recipe. She was a wonderful cook. My family and friends insist that I make it anytime we have a gathering.

Dorothy Mitchell Scott was a native of Andalusia, Alabama, and was married to Marvin (Buck) Scott for 37 years. They moved to Jay in 1983. She had six children: Anthony Lynn, Gina, Tammy, Sandy, Teresa, and Jason who all still reside in Jay. She was known in the community for her sewing skills. She passed away in November 2000 at 58 years old and is greatly missed by her family.

Dot's Potato Salad

4 lbs. Russet potatoes, cut up
5 eggs, boiled
1 cup sweet salad cubes
Salt & Pepper to taste
2 cups Dukes or Kraft Mayonnaise
1 Tbsp. Mustard

Boil cut-up potatoes in salted water until tender. Drain. Add chopped eggs, mayonnaise, mustard, and salad cubes. Add pepper and additional salt to taste. Add 1/2 chopped onion if desired.

Submitted by: Tammy Scott Linzy, daughter

Egg Drop Soup

Michael Xheng and Gracie Dong are the proprietors of New Jay Garden Chinese Restaurant. They migrated to Jay in 2009 from Missouri and New York.

1 qt. water
1/2 tsp. sugar
1 tsp. salt
1 tsp. chicken bouillon (flavored soup base mix)
1/4 tsp. white pepper
1- 1 1/2 tsp. of rice wine
1 drop of yellow food coloring
1 Tbsp. cornstarch
1 egg

Pour water in a large stock pot, bring to boil. Turn off stove, and mix in next 6 ingredients. Slowly stir in the cornstarch (this will cause your soup to thicken). Crack the egg in a separate container. Blend egg with a fork, and then slowly stir the egg into the soup mixture. (By pouring and stirring your egg at the same time, your egg will not clump).

Submitted by: Gracie Dong

Cream of Chicken Soup

Easy, quick comfort food from the home of Mary Evelyn and Barnett Hendricks

2 cans cream of mushroom soup
4 cups water
4 Tbsp. margarine
1 pint half and half
2 cans chicken broth
2 tsp. salt
4 cans white chicken
2 Tbsp. Chives, chopped
2 cups instant rice, uncooked

Put all ingredients in a pan and simmer for 30 minutes.

Submitted by: Mary Evelyn Hoomes Hendricks

Jeanette's Sweet Macaroni Salad

1 (16oz) pkg. elbow macaroni
1 lg. green pepper, chopped
2 cups mayonnaise
1 cup sugar
1 tsp. salt
4 med. carrots, shredded
1 med. red onion, chopped
1 can sweetened condensed milk
1 cup cider vinegar
1/2 tsp. pepper

Cook macaroni according to package directions; drain and rinse in cold water. In large serving bowl, combine the macaroni, carrots, green pepper, and onion. In a small bowl, whisk mayonnaise, milk, sugar, vinegar, salt, and pepper until smooth. Pour over macaroni mixture and toss to coat. Cover and refrigerate overnight.

Submitted by: Gail Lowry Deese, daughter

Ma's Old-Fashioned Chicken Soup

Our mother Cecile Penton, is 90 years old. She used to make this old timey, homemade soup in cold weather. Good to help cure colds and sinus problems.

1 whole cut up chicken   2 cups cornmeal

Add enough water to make small teaspoon round dumpling. Boil chicken in large pot of water until meat is done and falls off the bone. Remove chicken and all bones from broth. Cool chicken and cut or tear in to bite size pieces. Discard bones, skin, etc. add chicken back to pot of broth. Drop cornmeal by teaspoons, a few at a time to boiling mixture. Add salt and pepper to taste.

Submitted by: Joyce Penton Schnoor, daughter

Ura Bea's Broccoli Salad

4 cups of broccoli, chopped
1/2 cup green onions, chopped
1 cup of mayonnaise
1/3 cup of sugar
2 tsp. vinegar
1 cup celery, chopped
1 cup white grapes, cut in half.
1 cup, red grapes cut in half
 slivered almonds

Mix broccoli, onions, celery and grapes.
Mix mayonnaise, sugar, vinegar together and pour over vegetable and grape mixture. Top with almonds.

Submitted by: Glenda Hayes

Grandma Parker's 3-Day Cole Slaw

Euphemia Parker's Granddaughter Euphemia Miller Maddox's family in
the picture. John Maddox, wife Euphemia, son Clayton, and daughter
Cecile Maddox Penton

Grate a medium head of cabbage
Cut up one small Vidalia onion
Cut up one half of green Bell Pepper
Add one small jar of Pimento Pepper

Put next ingredients in a boiler together as follows:
1/2 cup of honey   1/2 cup white vinegar
1/2 cup cooking oil   2Tbsp. sugar
2 tsp. salt
Bring to hard boil, then pour over cut up vegetables and mix well. Let
set in refrigerator for three days in a covered container.

Submitted by: Joyce Penton Schnoor

Vera Boutwell's Apple Salad

Floyd Benjamin Boutwell & Bessie Austin Boutwell

This recipe was given to me and my Aunt Ann by my grandmother Vera Boutwell. It was actually her mother- in-law's recipe Bessie Austin Boutwell . Bessie along with her husband Floyd Benjamin Boutwell moved to Jay around 1900 from Alabama. They had ten children which included my grandfather Desmond Boutwell.

3 eggs	1 1/2 cups sweet milk
3/4 cup sugar	1 Tbsp vinegar
2 Tbsp. flour	1 cup pecans, chopped & toasted
4 cups of apples, chopped	

Mix sugar and flour together. Beat eggs, adding milk to eggs. Add to dry ingredients and cook slow until thickened. Add vinegar. Let cool. Add apples and pecans. Serve warm or chilled. Great with chicken!

Submitted by: Tami Brown, Granddaughter

24

Biscuits & Bread
of the
Great Pine Level

Frances Tanner Bowers
April 11, 1931 - December 19, 2010

On cold winter mornings, there was nothing better than waking up to the smell of bread baking. I'm sure cooking breakfast for a family of eight kept Momma on her toes. She would mix up the bread and have it in the oven before waking us. I can remember her singing, "School days, school days, good ole golden rule days," to wake us up. I remember coming to the table watching the butter melt on the bread and then pouring honey on it. The first bite was always the best. Warm, gooey, and sweet.

Leather Bread

3 cups self rising flour
2 Tbsp. oil
2 cups water
syrup or honey
butter

Mix flour, water, egg and 1 Tbsp. oil in large bowl. Grease 9 x12 baking pan, preheat oven to 350 degrees.

Pour flour mixture into pan, spread last tablespoon of oil over the top of the mixture. Bake for 30 minutes. Cut and serve hot with butter, honey or syrup.

Submitted by: Lori Bowers Brabham, daughter #4

Jane's Whipping Cream Biscuits

These biscuits are super easy and you can add any spice or dry ingredient you care and they will turn out fabulous!

2 cups self-rising flour (preferably White Lily, winter wheat)
1 cup of whipping or heavy cream

Combine ingredients in mixing bowl, stirring with fork until blended. (dough will be stiff). Turn dough out on floured surface and knead 10-12 times. Roll dough to 1/2 inch thickness and cut with 2 inch biscuit cutter.(I use a double old fashioned glass.)

Place on greased baking sheet. Cook at 450 degrees for 10-12 minutes. Makes about a dozen biscuits.

Submitted by: Jane Hayes

Mexican Cornbread

1/4 - 1/2 lb. cheese, grated
1 1/2 cups self rising cornmeal
1 can cream corn
1 small onion, chopped
1 egg
1 cup buttermilk
1/2 cup veg. oil
1 or 2 jalapenos, chopped

Grate cheese and set aside. In a bowl, mix all remaining ingredients well.
Place 1/2 of mixture in greased/sprayed 9x13 dish, layer all of cheese and then top with remaining mixture.
Bake at 400 degrees for about 45 minutes or until done.

Submitted by: Jane Hayes

Biscuit Toast

Dorothy Crews Penton

My Mom says she remembers that my grandmother would make this as a special treat back in Great Depression days.

Mom says a lot of "treats" were made with cane syrup because sugar was rationed back then.

Left over biscuits   A few pats of butter
Cane Syrup

Heat oven to 450 degrees. Split biscuits in half and place in oven proof pan or cast iron skillet. Cover with syrup and butter. Bake until brown and crispy on top.

Submitted by: Paula Penton Lewis, daughter

Carrie's Cracklin Cornbread

Carrie Lee Watson Floyd, born in 1910, and native of Geneva County, Alabama, moved to Jay in 1920 with parents John C. and Vertie Jane Watson, along with 8 siblings. They settled on Stockade Lane. Then in 1928, Carrie married Jimmy F. "Jack" Floyd and had 5 children; Jim, Shorty, Jerry, Janice and Roger.

1 1/2 cup plain cornmeal
2 Tbsp. flour
1 tsp. salt
2 eggs
1 Tbsp. hot oil
3/4 cup cracklins
1 cup plus milk or buttermilk

Mix meal, flour, powder and salt. Add rest of ingredients and mix well. May need to add a little extra milk. Grease skillet. Preheat oven to 400 degrees and put iron skillet in oven to preheat also. Pour batter into hot skillet and bake for 12 minutes plus, on bottom rack. Then put on top rack for browning. Serve hot.

Submitted by: Linda Hagler Floyd

Dr. Jim's Killer Arkansas Cornbread

In November of 2010 while at a hunting camp in Arkansas, I was appointed cook on a Tuesday morning as the mighty hunters left for their stands, my son-in-law said we want cornbread with pinto beans. I had never in my life cooked cornbread. So happened there was a bag of cornmeal on the table. I took the bag and read the recipe on it. I then made and inventory of the ingredients in the camp. The ingredients I couldn't find, I improvised. I did write down every step I took to cook the bread just in case it turned out.
I got rave reviews for the effort.

2 large eggs
2 cups self rising enriched yellow cornmeal mix
1 can whole kernel corn
1 cup buttermilk
1/2 cup of butter
2 tsp. sugar

Heat oven to 450 degrees. Coat cast iron skillet with bacon drippings (lard). Beat eggs in medium bowl, stir in rest of ingredients. and pour into prepared skillet. Bake 25-30 minutes or until golden brown. Cool in pans 10 minutes before serving.

Submitted by: Jimmy Lowry

Cecile's Hushpuppies

Cecile Penton, Joyce Schnoor and descendants

2 cups cornmeal (yellow or white)
2 Tbsp. flour
1 tsp. baking soda
1 tsp. baking powder
1 tsp. salt
1 lg. sweet onion, chopped
1 egg, beaten
1 cup buttermilk

Mix and sift dry ingredients together. Add chopped onion. Mix the beaten egg with the buttermilk. Add to dry ingredients. Drop by spoonfuls into hot grease. For extra good taste, fry hushpuppies in same oil where fish have been fried. When done, hushpuppies will float on top. Drain on brown paper and keep warm until ready to eat.

Momma's Buttermilk Biscuits & Cornbread

Rubye Elizabeth Hayes Butler

My mother put some of her recipes in a spiral bound steno pad with the title " Family Recipes from Rubye's Kitchen with My Love, Momma." She began writing them down when her health made it so that she could no longer stand on her feet to cook the food that she had spoiled my dad and our family with over many years. Mom loved to cook, and we all loved her cooking! As she wrote them down, she taught Dad to cook them for the two of them. He turned out to be a pretty good cook himself, but he doesn't like everyone to know because he doesn't enjoy showing off the talent she had taught him. Some of my favorite memories are Sunday afternoons. For as long as I can remember after I was grown, Mom and I would cook Sunday dinners together.

Momma's Buttermilk Biscuits

2/3 cups self rising flour
1/4 cup vegetable oil
1 cup buttermilk

Preheat oven to 450 degrees. Grease biscuit pan. Mix above ingredients together, using a large tablespoon drop spoonful of dough into bowl of flour. Cover with flour and form in palm of hand to form biscuit. Place biscuits in pan with sides touching. Bake until golden brown.

Momma's Buttermilk Cornbread

6 heaping Tbsp. of self rising cornmeal
1/4 cup vegetable oil
1 egg
Buttermilk

Preheat oven to 400 degrees. Recipe fits 9" iron skillet. Mix above ingredients together using a small amount of buttermilk and continue to add buttermilk until it reaches a thick pouring consistency. Pour into greased skillet (put grease in skillet and place in hot oven) once hot pour mix into hot skillet and place in oven. Bake till golden brown. About 25-30 minutes.

Submitted by: Cheryl Butler Johnson, daughter

The Best Mexican Cornbread

Janette Diamond

3 cups self rising cornmeal

3 eggs

1 ½ cups milk

1 cup oil

1 large onion, chopped

Jalapeño peppers, chopped (to taste)

1 ½ cups cheddar cheese, grated

3 Tbsp. sugar

1 can creamed corn

½ tsp. salt

Mix ingredients together. Bake in iron skillet at 400 degrees until brown.

Vegetables & Side Dishes
of the
Great Pine Level

Norman and Lena Ellis Sutton (1895– 1977)

I remember being in the kitchen with my grandmother cooking mustard greens on her old gas stove. Since I refused to eat mustard because it was bitter, Maw (as she was call by everyone) asked me what she could add that would make me like it. They say necessity is the mother of invention, and I guess that was the case with this, because by the time we finished adding my favorite ingredients to it, mustard greens became one of my favorite dishes.

Children:
Otis McCurley
O.T. Penton
Pauline Penton Fulmore
Edward Sutton

Country Quiche

1 large mess of fresh mustard greens
6 strips thinly sliced bacon
3 eggs
salt/pepper
1/2 cup shredded cheddar cheese

In a large cast iron skillet fry bacon strips until crisp.
Remove bacon and add mustard leaves. Cover and cook over medium
heat, stirring occasionally, for about 10 minutes. During this time you
can crush the crisp bacon strips. Remove cover and break eggs into
mustard. Stir mixture and continue cooking until eggs are done.
Add salt and black pepper to taste. Spread cheese over top and
sprinkle with crushed bacon.

Submitted by: Paula Penton Lewis, granddaughter

James and Mary Frances Hayes Hendricks

When I was away at Auburn and would come home on the weekends, my Grandma would fix me a big dish of this to take back with me on Sunday afternoons. It brings back a lot of good memories of time spent with her and is truly a "comfort food" of mine.

Mama Mary's Macaroni & Cheese

12 oz. macaroni, cooked
1 can cream of mushroom soup
1 cup mayonnaise
pinch of sugar
12 oz. cheddar cheese, grated
8 oz. sour cream
1 small jar pimento
Cheez-it crackers

Grease a large oblong oven dish. Mix mushroom soup, sour cream, mayonnaise, and pimento. Layer half macaroni, half cheese, and half soup mixture. Repeat layers. Crush enough Cheez-it crackers to cover the top and spread over the macaroni dish. Dot with butter. Bake at 350 degrees for 30-35 minutes or until crackers are slightly browned.
Will serve 12-16 people (or 2 hungry college roommates for a week).

Submitted by: Shanon Hendricks Kyser, granddaughter

Mary Nell Bowman McCaskill (1923-1981)

Mary Nell Bowman McCaskill (1923-1981)was a native of Bogia, Florida, graduating from Century High School in 1942. She married Jim McCaskill in the late 40's after Jim returned from WWII, so Jay became her home for the rest of her life. Nell and her husband raised six children on a small farm, so she spent many long hours harvesting, canning, and cooking their garden vegetables. Being an excellent cook, friends and relatives were always happy to sit down to one of the meals that she prepared. Nell served as pianist for Cora Baptist Church for over thirty years. Fishing was her favorite pastime, searching the river swamps with her best friend Jeanette for those perfect fishing spots.

She and her husband shared a reverence for Florida's natural beauty, loving its land and its resources.

Stewed Tomatoes & Okra

6 pieces of fried bacon, cut up
1 doz. okra pods
1 qt. fresh, peeled tomato wedges
1 med. onion, peeled & sliced thinly

Fry bacon in a skillet. Drain bacon slices. Reserve bacon grease. Sauté onions in bacon grease until transparent. Add fresh tomatoes and okra slices. Cook for about thirty minutes or until done. Add cut-up bacon pieces.

Candied Sweet Potatoes

6 lg. sweet potatoes
1 cup light brown sugar
2 tsp. vanilla
1 stick margarine

1 cup granulated sugar
2 Tbsp. flour
1 cup cold water

Parboil sweet potatoes. Peel potatoes and slice lengthwise thinly. Place potato slices in a buttered casserole dish. Mix other ingredients and cook until boiling, and then pour the mixture over the potatoes. Bake at 350 degrees for thirty minutes basting potatoes often with mixture.

Submitted by: Cynthia McCaskill Brook, daugther

Dr. Jim's Killer Baked Bean Recipe

This bean recipe came from what was in the kitchen the first time I ever made baked beans. It seems to work, so I didn't change it!

2- 28 oz. cans of Bush's original style beans
2 cups ketchup
1/4 cup of Sweet Baby Ray's BBQ sauce
1 Tbsp. French's mustard
salt and pepper, to taste
1 onion, chopped
1/2 pod of bell pepper, chopped
Juice of 1/2 lemon
1/4 cup sweet pickle juice
1/2-1 lb. bacon, latticed on top

Chop veggies and stir into beans with all ingredients.
Fry bacon in butter, drain excess fat, and set aside.
Pour beans in to Dutch oven, place bacon on top, and cook until the beans reach a temp of 165 degrees.

Submitted by: Jimmy Lowry

Paw-Paw's Squash Casserole

J. Haynes "Paw-Paw" Brabham

This is a favorite at the annual Brabham Family Reunion that is held in Enterprise, Alabama each Thanksgiving. Haynes grew up in a large family (8 brothers and sisters) and his dad died at a young age so all the boys had to learn to cook too!

2 med. squash
1/2 cup bell pepper, finely chopped
1 egg
1 cup bread crumbs
1/2 cup onion, finely chopped
1 cup milk
Dash of black pepper
1/4 cup butter

Peel and slice squash. Cook until tender in boiling salted water. Drain and mash squash into small pieces with a fork. Add chopped onion and bell pepper. Beat egg slightly, combine with milk, black pepper, and cracker crumbs and add to squash. Pour mixture into a greased casserole. Dot with butter and bake at 350 degrees, 30-40 minutes.
Variation: Use cheese crackers as an added top layer when baking.

Submitted by: Lori Bowers Brabham, daughter-in-law

Charline's Corn Casserole

2 eggs
1/4 cup milk
1/2 cup cracker crumbs
1 can cream style corn
1/4 cup melted butter
1/4 cup grated carrot
2 Tbsp. celery, chopped
1 Tbsp. onion, chopped
1/8 tsp. hot sauce
1/2 tsp. sugar
1/2 tsp. salt
1/2 cup shredded cheddar cheese

Combine eggs and milk, beat until well blended. Add cracker crumbs and set aside until all liquid if absorbed. Add remaining ingredients, except cheese to cracker crumb mixture, stirring well. Spoon mixture in to greased 1 qt. casserole dish. Bake at 350 degrees for 45 minutes. Sprinkle with cheese while hot

Submitted by: Judy Baker Flowers, granddaughter

Mary Evelyn's Tater Tot Casserole

32 oz. bag frozen Tater Tots
1 lb. ground beef, browned
2 14 1/4 oz. cans Green beans, drained
10 oz. can of cream mushroom soup
1 Tbsp. dried onions
1/4 cup milk
salt & pepper to taste

Line slow cooker/crockpot with frozen tater tots. Mix remaining ingredients together. pour over tater tots, cover. Cook on high 3 hours. Sprinkle individual servings with grated cheese.

Submitted by: Mary Evelyn Hendricks

Squash Casserole

1 lb. squash
1 small onion, chopped
2 eggs beaten
1 cup bread crumbs
3 Tbsp. butter
1 cup milk
1 cup grated cheese
Salt & Pepper to taste

Combine squash and onions, cook, drain and mash. Add remaining ingredients reserving 1/2 cup of cheese to sprinkle over top. Pour into buttered casserole dish. bake at 375 degrees until firm and cheese is brown.

Submitted by: Billie Faye Cannon Smith

Argie Ruth's Vegetables

Argie Ruth Shiver Bragg

My mother Argie Ruth Shiver Bragg was a wonderful cook. She was best at cooking vegetables. Mother's new potatoes and English peas were so good in the spring of the year. It would take a large garden to grow English peas. Daddy did not plant very many rows of them, so there would only be a few to pick. Mother would make them go farther by cooking them with scraped new potatoes, OH SO GOOD!

New Potatoes & English Peas
Pick peas and shell.
Dig new potatoes, wash and scrape.

Bring new potatoes to boil, adding salt and pepper and when almost done, add English peas and continue cooking until all are done. Add butter. Make thickening sauce by add milk to flour. Slowly add to hot potatoes and peas until you thicken to your liking.

Mother's Stewed Squash

Wash squash, slice and place in iron skillet, cover with water. Bring to boil, cover and cook until tender. Remove cover and cook until water is cooked out, stirring and mashing squash. Add salt, pepper, diced onions, and cooking oil. Cook until done.

Mother's Corn

We always enjoyed her fresh or frozen corn. We could never tell the difference between them. Mother used the field corn that daddy grew. Daddy would go out early in the morning and gather a truckload of the corn. Mother would be getting the washtubs ready with ice water to put the corn in when it was silked. By the time daddy returned from the field, mother would be ready. Daddy would shuck the corn and mother would start silking it. By this time, my Grandmother Shiver would be coming from her house next door with her dishpan and sharp knife to begin cutting the corn off the cob. When daddy was through shucking the corn, his part was done until it was cooked and on the table. Mother did not blanche her corn; she kept it cold and put it in bags quickly and froze it. You could not tell if it was fresh or frozen!

Put fresh corn in iron skillet. Add seasoning (bacon drippings) salt, pepper, tablespoon of sugar, and water. Bring to boil. Add water as needed as corn will thicken. Cook on low heat until done to taste.

Submitted by: Angeline Bragg Andrews, daughter

Grace's Vegetables

Fletcher & Grace Hoomes

Turnip & Dumplin's- Living out in the country as I was growing up, mama would cook a large pot of fresh Turnips and add these dumplings. I remember coming in from school and the pot would still be on the stove. I would get a plate and eat away!

- Mary Evelyn Hoomes Hendricks

A Corny Story - Grace Hoomes
I grew up on a small farm where Papa plowed with a mule and all us kids did most of the farm work by hand. On one occasion, my brothers and sisters and I were picking cotton. While doing so, we decided to place a game of who could tell the "biggest story." The winner would not have to pick cotton and could wait for the others in the shade. My younger brother, Hayes was the winner.
His "story" was about Pa Pebbles' mule that was kept in the barn.

Popcorn was stored in the loft above the mule. It was an extremely hot August day and the popcorn began to "pop" and fall down on the mule. According to Hayes, the mule thought the popcorn was snow and froze to death!

Cornmeal Dumplings in Turnips

2 cups cornmeal
1 Tbsp. flour
1/2 tsp. salt
pinch of baking soda
1/4 tsp. baking powder

Sift all ingredients together (except turnips). Mix with water until stiff consistency. Roll in to small balls and drop on top of turnip greens that are almost done. There needs to be a lot of pot liquor in the greens, and it will soak in to the dumplings. They won't be brown, but sort of firm and a little sticky. Cook 30 minutes or until done.

Submitted by: Mary Evelyn Hoomes Hendricks

Baked Corn

1 can whole kernel corn, drained
1 can cream style corn
3 oz. sour cream
1 cup butter, melted
2 eggs , slightly beaten
1 12oz. Pkg. of corn muffin mix

Preheat oven to 350 degrees. Combine all ingredients. Mix well. Pour in to 9x13 baking dish. Bake 35-45 minutes.

Submitted by: Rachel Hoomes Hendricks

Grandma Robert's Candied Yams

Jack W. and Betty Gulsby Roberts (1891-1978)

6-8 medium baked sweet potatoes
1 stick butter
1 cup brown sugar
1 cup sugar
1 tsp. vanilla
1 tsp. cinnamon
Pecans

Slice potatoes in half and arrange in casserole dish. Melt butter in saucepan and cook over low heat until sugar dissolves, stirring constantly. Add vanilla and cinnamon. Pour over potatoes. Sprinkle with pecans. Bake at 300 degrees for 15-20 minutes.

Submitted by: Becky Jones, granddaughter

Marilyn's Easy Cajun Rice

Marilyn Whaley

1 can each: French Onion Soup, Cream of Mushroom, Cream of Chicken

1 med. bell pepper
1 bunch of green onions, (heads & tails)
3/4 lb. ground chuck
3/4 lb. sausage (hot or mild)
1 1/2 cups uncooked rice

Throw all these raw ingredients in a metal or glass baking dish and mix well. Season with Tony Chachere's or what ever you have. Cover with foil and put in a 400 degree oven for 1 1/2 hours or until rice is done.

Mashed Tatties and Neeps

Robert & Miriam Ingram

Miriam Hudgens Ingram is the wife of Robert Ingram. She moved to Jay in 1949 when her father became pastor of Jay United Methodist Church. She and Robert have two children: Terry Ingram of Memphis, Tennessee and Cynthia (Cindy) Tebbetts of Prattville, Alabama. She and Robert have 4 grandsons.

1lb. potatoes	1/4 tsp. salt
1 lg. rutabaga, (2 lbs.)	1/4 tsp. pepper
1/4 cup butter or margarine	3/4 cup warm milk

Pare & quarter potatoes & rutabaga; cut rutabaga in to 1 inch cubes. Place potatoes & rutabagas in large saucepan. Cover with water & bring to a boil. Reduce heat to low, cover and simmer 20-25 minutes until vegetables are soft. Then drain them & discard water.
With mixer on low speed, beat vegetables with butter; gradually beat in milk until mixture is smooth. Season with salt & pepper.

Pineapple Casserole

Emma Ruth Cannon

2 (20 oz.) cans chunk or tidbit pineapple, drained (set juice aside)
2 cups cheddar cheese, shredded
3/4 cup sugar
6 Tbsp. all-purpose flour
6 Tbsp. pineapple juice

Topping: 1 stick of butter & 1 tube of Ritz crackers
Stir together sugar and flour. Add juice. Mix pineapple and cheese.
Pour into a greased 9 x12 dish. Bake at 350 degrees for 15 minutes.
Crush crackers, mix with melted butter. Pour over the above and bake
for 15 minutes longer for a perfect crust.

Rochelle's Tomato Gravy

Rochelle Walters Arnette

1/4 cup flour
1/4 cup hog lard (any grease/oil will do)
1 tsp. salt
1 quart of whole milk (more or less until gravy is desired thickness)

Melt lard over a warm fire and stir in flour. Add salt. Stir constantly until blended and slightly browned. Slowly add the milk, stirring constantly so that mixture does not lump. Stir in a jar of tomatoes and simmer. Serve over hot biscuits.

Submitted by: Dorothy Arnette Diamond, daughter

Rose's Southern Fried Okra

Rose Brown Harris was my mother and as far back as I can remember this was one of my favorite things to eat. As un-enjoyable as
the process of cutting okra from the garden was, the deliciousness of the
food made up for the effort. Mama's fried okra was enjoyed by many
at the various family events and dinners on the ground at Pine Level
Baptist Church. Rose was married to Fletcher Harris, and they had
two children: Judy, who passed away as a child and Shirley. Rose and
Fletcher lived on Highway 89 in the Pine Level Community.

Rose's Southern Fried Okra

About 50 small to medium fresh okra
½ cup plain flour
½ cup yellow cornmeal
½ tsp. salt
½ tsp. black pepper
1 egg
2 Tbsp. milk
Oil for frying
Paper towels

Wash okra. Trim ends. Slice in ½ inch thick pieces.

In a mixing bowl, combine flour, cornmeal, salt and pepper. Mix well. In another bowl, beat together egg and milk.

Dip okra into the egg mixture, and then dip into the cornmeal mixture. Be sure okra is coated well.

Fry part of the coated okra in deep skillet with about ½ inch hot oil. Watch closely during frying process and turn frequently. After a few minutes, remove fried okra with slotted spoon and drain on paper towels placed on plate.

Put more okra in and fry. Continue process until all okra is fried and drained. Transfer all drained okra from plate to serving bowl. Serve hot and enjoy.

Submitted by: Shirley Harris Pyritz ,daughter

Fletcher's Mixed Greens

Fletcher said "Your food is going to get mixed up in your stomach any-
way. You might as well save some time and mix it up on your plate or
in your cooking."

Fletcher Harris was my dad. My mom passed away with cancer,
and he and I began a search of looking for lifestyle changes that could
make one healthier and less susceptible to cancer. One finding was to
increase the number of servings of vegetables eaten in a day and to prepare those vegetables in a manner other than the frying we are used to
in the South.

Being a very determined individual, Fletcher changed the foods he ate
and the manner in which they were prepared. There is a saying that "an
old dog can't learn new tricks," but Fletcher dispelled that myth by
making these changes after reaching his 80th birthday.

After I moved to Pensacola and he become solely responsible for his
food preparation, he cut to the chase and prepared his vegetables together, instead of preparing the broccoli and then preparing the collards
or mustard greens in a separate dish. He lived independently until the
age of 92. He was a farmer, and our family lived on Highway 89 in the
Pine Level community.

Fletcher's Mixed Greens

1 pkg. 10 – 16 ounces frozen broccoli
1 pkg. 10 – 16 ounces frozen collards
1 Tbsp. olive oil
Salt and pepper to taste

Heat oil in skillet. Sautee broccoli and collards for a few minutes until tender. When ready to remove from heat, season with salt and pepper.

This was a favorite of Fletcher's and he changed the recipe by using different types of greens (such as mustard greens or turnip greens) and by adding additional vegetables such as cauliflower, carrots, etc.

During the summer, if using fresh vegetables that take longer to cook, add some water and prepare in a pot on your stove top or in a steamer instead of in a skillet. Fletcher ate some variation of this dish almost every day for over ten years and he lived to be 92. He thought this was a tasty and easy way to get your daily vegetables.

Submitted by: Shirley Harris Pyritz, daughter

Meat and Game
of the
Great Pine Level

James Mack "Jim" McCaskill **(1921-1999)** was a life-long
resident of Jay, Florida. He enjoyed playing basketball at Jay High
School and graduated in 1940. He served the U.S. Army during the latter part of WWII. He enjoyed farming his family's estate for most of his
life, but in his later career, he served as foreman for the District III Santa Rosa County Road Department, retiring in 1989. Jim was an avid
fisherman and hunter. He loved the rivers, woods and swamps of Santa
Rosa and Escambia counties. He was a descendant of some of the first
1770's Scot's Bend settlers of this area. He was a member of VFW,
American Legion Post #121, and an honorary member of the Williams'
Lake Hunting Club. He was married to Mary Nell Bowman McCaskill,
and they had six children: Jimmy, Cynthia, Rosemary, Larry, Gary, and
Jeff. Daddy always said that eating squirrel or cow brains was guaran-
teed to make you smart. I guess that's why many of his friends nick-
named him "Brainy"

Daddy's Deep Fried Squirrel Heads

12 freshly skinned and cleaned squirrel heads with eyeballs removed
4 cups of cooking oil
salt and pepper to taste
2-3 cups flour

Salt and pepper each squirrel head. Roll each head separately in a bowl of flour. Heat cooking oil in a cast iron frying pan. Place floured heads in hot cooking oil. Fry heads for 10 minutes, turning them over after cooking for 5 minutes. Drain cooked heads on a paper towel.

To eat contents of the head, crack the skull open with a sturdy utensil, such as the back of a heavy spoon. Squirrel heads are enjoyed best by just sucking the brain matter out of the head.

Submitted by: Cynthia McCaskill Brock, daughter

Jimmy Lowry

This is a rub I developed over a period of a few years. The combination of ingredients seem to work well together. When preparing the rub, grind the ingredients as fine as you can.

I always prepare the rub two days before I need it. This gives it time to mellow, and the flavors to come together.

Dr. Jim's Dry Rib Rub Recipe

1 cup sea salt
1 cup black pepper
1/4 cup ground coriander
1 cup ground cumin
1 cup smoked paprika
1 cup dried thyme
1 cup chili powder
2 lbs. dark brown sugar
Apple juice
Sweet Baby Ray's BBQ Sauce
Ribs

Mix dry rub ingredients all together.
Wash ribs and marinate in apple juice for 10 hours. Apply even coat of the rub on the meat side of the ribs and let marinate 12 hours.
Apply a light coat of Sweet Baby Ray's BBQ Sauce on the meat side of the ribs when placing into the smoker. Set temp to 225 degrees and do not open until the internal temp reaches 170 degrees.
Serve with Sweet Baby Ray's BBQ Sauce.

Submitted by: Jimmy Lowry

Lilian and John Cashman

Lilian Kobus Cashman was my paternal grandmother. She was of
German descent and a native of South Dakota. Everyone called her
"Lil." In 1933 she married John Cashman. He was of English/Irish
descent and a native of Wisconsin. His job relocated him to Minnesota
where they lived out the rest of their lives. Lil was a dedicated
Homemaker. She had many talents and excelled in all of them. I
remember her best for her love of baking. Her brownies and cookies
were the best. One of my best memories was the year before she
died she introduced my family to camping. I have great memories of
Her, and today some of her favorite recipes are my favorites, too.

Lilian Cashman's Pheasant

Fresh Pheasant
salt and pepper to taste
2 cups of milk (2% or whole) or sub with 1 1/2 cups milk and 1/2 cup
of cream.

After cleaning pheasant. wash and cut off wings. Split the back, leave
back whole. Salt and pepper to taste. Brown butter in skillet (best in
large skillet) Add milk. Cover and cook in oven for 45 minutes or until
tender at 325 degrees. Keep moist, baste often

Submitted by: Rick J. Cashman, grandson

Cassie Arizona Wright Diamond

Cassie Diamond, known to her family as "Mama Diamond," was a wonderful cook. Cassie was born in Randolph County, Alabama, in 1898, and she learned to cook at an early age. Eating at her table was always a wonderful, delectable experience. She and "Papa Diamond" loved having company to eat with them. Her children, grand-children, and their friends in the town of Jay always found something good to eat in her kitchen.

Mama Diamond's Chili Pork Chops

6 center cut pork chops
1 large bell pepper
1 large onion
2 bottles of chili sauce

Brown pork chops over medium heat in a small amount of oil. Keep all pork chops in the pan. Peel and slice onion and lay slices on top of pork chops. Seed and cut bell pepper into rings and lay on top of onion. Pour all of chili sauce over pepper, onion and chops. Cover and cook over low heat until pork chops are tender. Serve over cooked rice.

Submitted by: Marshall Diamond, son

Daddy's Boiled Chitterlings "Chitlins"

My memories of the preparation and cooking of this dish are all terrible.
I can remember watching Daddy and one of his friends wash fresh hog
intestines in the creek below our house. I would stand high on the creek
bank, heaving through the nauseating process, as I watched them
painstakingly clean those pale, long, unending, ruffled hog intestines.
The sickening sight of what was coming out of them was even worse,
as I watched the contents float down the creek.

It seemed to me that Daddy would only cook them on Friday or
Saturday night at the exact time that my date was supposed to pick me
up. All through the lengthy cooking process, as the odor of hog poop
permeated the house. I would beg my daddy to let me meet my boy-
friend outside to no avail, for that was against my parent's rules. My
date would always have to come inside to speak to my parents. The
embarrassment of having him come inside a house that reeked of
cesspool odors lingered with me and on me through the night. I never
understood how daddy could get past the repulsive smell of those
ghastly, gnarly things and even eat them. but evidently, he loved them,
or maybe he just loved trying to get rid of my boyfriends.

10 lbs. cleaned chitterlings

2 tsp. salt

1 tsp. crushed red pepper flakes

1 lg. onion

1/2 tsp. black pepper

1 tsp. garlic, minced

Soak the chitterlings (pig intestines) in cold water throughout the
cleaning stage. Each chitterling should be examined and run under cold
Water. All foreign materials should be removed and discarded.
Chitterlings should retain some fat, so be careful to leave some while
washing. After each chitterling has been cleaned, soak in two coldwater
baths for a few minutes. The second water bath should be clearer, if not,
soak in one more bath.

Place chitterlings in a six-quart pot and fill with cold water. Bring to a
boil, and then add the onion. Season with salt, garlic, and red pepper
flakes. Be sure the water is at a full boil before adding seasonings, or
the chitterlings could become tough. Continue to simmer for 3-4 hours,
depending on how tender you like them. Once the chitterlings are done,
remove from heat and cut into one-inch pieces. May server over rice
and top with a sprinkling of vinegar or hot sauce.

Submitted By: Cynthia McCaskill Brock, daughter

Robert's Wild Card Chili

Robert always makes a triple cooking of this, and we serve it with grilled cheese sandwiches.

1 lb. of hamburger
1/2 chopped onion
1 can red beans
1 can refried beans
1 8oz can tomato sauce
1 cup water
1/2 tsp. salt
1/2 tsp. garlic salt
1/8 tsp. black pepper
1/8 tsp. cayenne pepper
3 Tbsp. chili powder
1 Tbsp. molasses

Brown hamburger with onions in a Dutch oven. Pour off fat. Add remaining ingredients, cover, and simmer for 1 hour. Stir occasionally.

Submitted by: Cecelia Hayes, wife

Hubert Lowry's 4th of July Barbequed Goat

Hubert Lowry

Hubert Lowry & Cassie Morris were married in 1932 and raised 14 children. Total descendants today equal 132. Hubert was a farmer, a dairyman, and later worked as a deputy sheriff and a state meat inspector. It was a tradition for Hubert to barbeque a goat for the 4th of July family get-together each year. The photo above is of Hubert with eight of his fourteen children

The two hind quarters and the shoulders of a goat were seasoned and basted with barbeque sauce.
An old refrigerator hull with a hole cut through the top to let smoke escape provided the smoker. Smoke also escaped around the closed door. Only hickory wood could be used and a very low temperature maintained. The four quarters of the goat were hung from the top of the smoker and cooked all night. Every two or three hours, more sauce would be applied to the meat to keep it from drying out. Early on the Fourth, the meat was taken out of the smoker and cut for serving. It was always very tender and delicious.

Marshall's Camp Stew

Marshall Diamond

1 lb. ground beef or venison
1 can whole kernel corn, drained
1 med. onion, chopped
1 green pepper, chopped
1 can pork & beans
1 can English peas, drained
1/4 cup cane syrup or honey

Brown venison/beef in large pot and drain. Add onions & pepper; cook slightly. Add pork & beans, corn, & English peas. Stir in syrup & simmer until onions and pepper are done. Serve with crackers or cornbread.

Pattie's Corned Beef with Mustard Sauce

Pattie Gerber & Jackie Gerber Stewart-Ard

My parents Pattie and Fred Gerber met during WWII when my dad was on R and R and recovering from malaria. He was sent to New Zealand, which is where my mom was born and reared. They fell in love and got married within three weeks of meeting. My dad was sent back in the war, and they did not see one another for 3 long years. The next time they saw each other was when the ship that brought my mom to the states docked in San Francisco. She could not get off the ship until the next day and he could not board the ship, so they just stood there looking at one another. The next day they started the long journey to Seattle, Washington, which was where my dad had grown up. I came along later and my parents decided that after my brother Bruce came along that they wanted to live in a warmer climate. We moved to Southern California, and finally to Santa Rosa, California, which is only fifty miles north of San Francisco. During the time we lived in southern California, we went to New Zealand for three months. My Grandfather had died, and my mom needed to take care of some things. My mom's mother died when my mom was 15 and she had gone to live with an aunt, as young ladies needed the proper upbringing that a man could not provide.

I met and married George Haywood Stewart while he was stationed in California at a small base called Two Rock. I was working for State Farm Regional office and some of my fellow workers had invited me to a party they were having. I made a new dress, and drove my brand new VW Bug to the party. It took a couple of months before we started dating, I was going out with his roommate and friend, all the while wishing I could go out with him. Once we started to date, we would go out every night with a group of friends an on the weekends we would go to the beach or river for picnics. After we were married for a couple of months he got out of the service and we came to Jay. It was a big change for me, as I was used to many stores, and most businesses stayed open until 10 p.m.. Some were open all night; and the radio stations stayed on 24 hours a day. When I first came to Jay everything closed at 5 p.m. You can imagine my surprise when the radio signed off at 5 p.m.!

Submitted by: Jackie Gerber Stewart-Ard, daughter

Corned Beef:

1 onion, quartered	1 stalk of celery
1 bay leaf	1 tsp. dill seed
1 tsp. mustard seeds	4 peppercorns

Put all in a pot with corned beef (rinsed before placing in pot). Cover with cold water. Cook slowly at a simmer for 3 hours. When finished cooking make mustard sauce and serve.

Mustard Sauce for Corned Beef:

1 cup beef pot liquor	1/4 cup cider vinegar
1 large (rounded)	tsp. dry mustard
1 Tbsp. butter	2 Tbsp. all purpose flour
1/4 cup sugar	1 egg

Beat egg in a pot. Add all other ingredients. Stir in pot liquor last. Stir over medium heat until thick. Do not boil. Once thick pour into a smaller pitcher. Serve with sliced corned beef and enjoy.

Will Nelson's Bear Stew

Will Nelson

During the late 1800's and early 1900's bear were plentiful along the rivers and creeks of Santa Rosa County. Will Nelson was the son of James Nelson and his wife, Julia Ann McCormick Nelson. Will (my Granny Daisy Nelson Penton's brother) is shown kneeling down and petting his dog after killing a good size bear near Escambia River in North Santa Rosa County.

Bear Stew made with meat, potatoes, tomatoes, and other vegetables from the garden, seasoned with salt and pepper made a good meal.

Note: Bears, Panthers, & Gophers are now protected , so be aware of this law when you go hunting.

Submitted by: Joyce Penton Schnoor, grand niece

Truss' Boiled Squirrel Stew

Truss Shell

4 squirrels, dressed
4 tsp. salt
4 tsp. black pepper
2 pods Red (HOT) pepper

½ cup grease
2-3 pieces fresh ham or deer meat
2-3 large onions, cut into small pieces

Put 1 ½ gallons cold water in a heavy metal pot. Put the 4 squirrels in the pot of water and bring to a quick boil, then skim. Cover and continue boiling for approximately 30 minutes. Then add remaining ingredients to the pot. Continue boiling for at least another 30 minutes or until meat is tender. Serve with light bread and baked sweet potatoes.

Old Fashioned Spicy Chili

Richard and Dixie Carlton

2 lbs. lean ground beef	1 ½ Tbsp. sugar
1 med onion, chopped	2 – 16 oz. Cans kidney beans, un-drained
4 cloves garlic, minced	16 oz. can whole tomatoes, chopped
2 Tbsp. ground cumin	6 oz. can tomato paste
2 tsp. salt	1 can hot chili beans
4-6 Tbsp. chili powder	2 Tbsp. all-purpose flour

Combine first 5 ingredients in a large Dutch oven. Cook over medium heat, stirring to crumble meat, until it's all brown and onions are tender. DRAIN- off pan drippings. Stir in chili powder, flour, and sugar. Add remaining ingredients, stirring well. Mixture will be thick. Cover and simmer for 30 minutes over low heat.

Deep Fried Rattlesnake

1 rattlesnake, cut into 3" pieces
2 Tbsp. Lemon juice
¼ cup oil
1 tsp. salt
Fritter Batter
Oil

Marinate meat in refrigerator overnight in lemon juice, ¼ cup oil & salt. Baste meat occasionally. Wipe meat dry. Dip in fritter batter. Deep fry in heavy skillet.

Fritter Batter

1 egg   ½ cup milk
½ cups plus 1- 2 Tbsp. self rising flour

Beat egg and milk together; stir in flour. Let batter rest 20 minutes. Batter should be quite runny, like fresh cream, when used. Only a thin batter will fry crisp.

Barbequed Armadillo

1 armadillo   Bacon grease
1 cup butter   ½ cup ketchup
½ cup grated onion   2 Tbsp. mustard
Tabasco to taste
Or use your favorite BBQ sauce

In sauce pan, combine butter, ketchup, onion, mustard and tabasco. Heat over low heat until butter is melted. Stir occasionally.

Rub bacon grease into the armadillo. Grill over a hot fire for 5 minutes, reduce fire by half. Baste the meat with sauce until done. Armadillo is cooked like Pork. Serve and enjoy!

Fish & Seafood
of the
Great Pine Level

Bessie Kelley's Shrimp Gumbo

Bessie Kelley

1 lb. raw shrimp	½ tsp. Pepper
3 Tbsp. melted fat	2 cups hot water
2 cups sliced okra	1 cup tomatoes
½ cup chopped onion	2 whole bay leaves
2 cloves garlic	½ tsp. pepper sauce
1 ½ tsp. salt	1 ½ cups cooked rice

Peel & devein shrimp. Place fat in large frying pan. When melted, add okra and sauté for 10 minutes or until somewhat dry. Stirring constantly, add onion, garlic, salt, pepper, and shrimp. Cook 5 minutes. Add water, tomatoes, bay leaves, and pepper sauce. Cover and simmer for 20 minutes.

Creamy Fettuccine Alfredo - Shrimp or Chicken

1 cup (2 sticks) butter, softened
2 cups, grated Parmesan cheese
Fresh basil leaves
2 cups whipping cream
1 (1lb.) box of Fettuccine
1/8 tsp. salt
1/8 tsp. black pepper

Place butter in a large heatproof bowl. Using a wooden spoon, or an electric mixer set on low speed, beat until smooth. Add the cream and Parmesan cheese. Stir until well blended; set aside.
Bring large saucepan of lightly salted water to a boil. Add the pasta and cook according to package directions. Drain well and immediately add the hot pasta to the butter mixture in the large bowl. Using two forks, toss the fettuccine in the butter mixture to coat well. Add the salt and pepper.
Divide the pasta between 4 serving plates. Quickly slice the basil in to shreds to equal 1/4 cup. Sprinkle shredded basil over each serving. We also add rotisserie chicken chopped or shrimp that has been shelled, deveined and sautéed.

Submitted by: Glenda Henderson Hayes

Lillie Griffis & James Monroe Elliot

My Parents, Lillie (Griffis) and James Monroe Elliot were born in Santa Rosa Co. Florida. She was reared in Mt. Carmel and he was in Milton and Pensacola. I learned that they were introduced to fishing at an early age and continued to enjoy it throughout their lives. If they went fishing, we could expect a fish fry upon their return, and if the catch was plentiful, the rest of the family would be invited. If they fished in Jay, it would be freshwater fish, and Lil's family. If in Pensacola, it was saltwater fish and crabs to boot. In addition, the fishing party would be larger. This meant more seafood and a bigger
fish fry/party! It was always good, clean, family fun.

In 1952, James returned to the Navy. His career always put us somewhere on the coast with lots of places to fish. Charleston, S.C. , Portsmouth, Va. and while stationed in Maryland we would crab in the Chesapeake Bay.. A crab boil was always on the agenda because the "blue crab" were outstanding. Many times our return trip to visit family would include a fishing trip and fish fry. The family recipe liked by all was this.

Lillie & James' Crab Jambalaya

Sauce:
1 lg. onion, diced per dozen crabs
4 large cloves of garlic diced
3 Tbsp. Sweet Basil
1 large can tomato paste
2 Tbsp. Gumbo File'
1 can tomatoes
2 stalks celery
1 large can tomato puree
1 bell pepper
2 Tbsp. parsley flakes
2 Tbsp. Worcestershire Sauce

Start by browning onions and garlic in a little butter or oil. Add remaining ingredients and simmer. Add sauce to crabs and cooked rice (1 1/2 cups rice per dozen crabs) and serve!
Note: Fresh shrimp may be used instead of Crabs.

Submitted by: Patricia Elliott Cashman, daughter

Marilyn's Easy Shrimp Dish

1 lb. shrimp
2 cans cream of mushroom soup
1 can Rotel (tomatoes & peppers)
1 bunch of green onions, chopped
2 Tbsp. garlic, minced
1 stick of butter

Sauté green onions in 1 stick of butter. Add shrimp and sauté. Add 2 cans of cream of mushroom soup. Add 1 can of rotel, simmer for 20 minutes and serve over rice.

Submitted By: Marilyn Whaley

Red Snapper Stew

5 lbs. Red Snapper
2 1/2 lbs. onions, sauté in butter
3 sticks of celery
2 lbs. potatoes
1 pint of stewed fresh squash, cut
2 lg. cans chopped tomatoes
Salt
Pepper
Red pepper

In large boiler, put sautéed onions and boil fish in water until done and debone. Return fish to boiled with remaining celery, cut up potatoes, tomatoes, and squash. Put sprinkle of red pepper and black pepper. Add salt to taste. Boil until done and serve over rice.
Note: this broth will boil down but not thicken.

Submitted by: Gladys Cobb Hagler

Helen West Crews' Crab Gumbo

Helen West Crews

Helen West of the Jay area West clan, married Emery Crews of Allentown. She & Emery had 2 children Charles Calvin Crews & Sharon Elizabeth Crews Solis.

Ingredients:
2 dozen fresh crabs, washed/dressed/split

1 lrg can whole tomatoes	3/4 cup flour
1 med. sweet onion	1/2 cup vegetable oil
2 cans tomato sauce	1 can tomato paste
4 cups cooked rice	Salt & Pepper to taste

Dress & wash crabs; set aside on ice. Brown flour in oil. Bring 2 gallons of water to boil; add tomatoes, tomato sauce, paste and chopped onion. Bring back to boil. Add roux (flour & oil mixture). Stir lightly, returning again to boil. Add crabs. Bring to boil let cook 10 minutes, boiling continuously. Serve over cooked rice.

J.O.'s Turtle Soup

J.O. (OL) Cobb and Ila Mae Pugh Cobb were married in 1930. They lived at Cobbtown and had three children; Gladys Hagler, Floyd Cobb and Helen Bray. "OL" had many fishing buddies, one was Grover "Dunk" McKenzie. They would catch either Loggerhead or soft-shell turtle to make this soup.

1 extra large loggerhead turtle
1 cup flour
Water
Salt & pepper

Clean and cut up turtle. Boil in large thick boiler until tender. Remove bones. Mix flour with a little water until thick. Roll dough on floured surface until thin. Pinch off extra small pieces or use a pizza roller, floured to cut in small pieces. Flour these extra good, so they won't stick to each other. Put into boiling broth and turtle. Salt and pepper to taste. Simmer on low heat until thick. Some of the dough dumplings will turn in to part of the broth and be thick.

Oyster Stew

Gladys Cobb Hagler born in 1932 married Buford Hagler in 1950. They had four children; Gary, Linda Floyd, Terry, and Pam Matheny. They also had six grandchildren & eight great-grandchildren. she was a great cook andalways had plenty when visitors came in.

1 qt. fresh oysters, drained
1 tsp. salt
Sprinkle of red pepper
Dash of black pepper
2 Tbsp. of butter
4 cups of fresh milk

Clean heavy broiler, put all ingredients except oysters, on top of stove and heat to a boil. DO NOT BOIL. Add oysters, and stir until texture changes. Serve while hot.

Wallace's Shrimp Creole

Wallace Diamond

¼ cup salad oil

1 cup onion, thinly sliced

1 cup celery, thinly sliced

1 cup bell pepper, strips 2" long

3 ½ cups canned tomatoes

8 oz. can tomato sauce

2 bay leaves

1 Tbsp. sugar

1 Tbsp. salt

1 Tbsp. chili powder

1/8 tsp. Tabasco sauce

2 lbs. raw cleaned, shrimp

2 Tbsp. flour

1/3 cup water

Preheat electric skillet to 300 degrees. Pour in oil, and sauté onions, celery, and bell pepper until tender, but not brown. Add tomatoes, tomato sauce, bay leaves, sugar, salt, chili powder,& Tabasco sauce; mix well. Add shrimp. Cover and reduce temperature. Simmer 30 minutes or longer. Mix flour and water. Add to mixture and cook about 5 minutes until thickened. Serve over rice.

Debbie's Okra Shrimp Creole

Debra Ross Hayes

¾ cup bell pepper, chopped

1 large onion, chopped

2½ tsp. sugar

¼ tsp. hot sauce

¼ tsp. cayenne pepper

2 Tbsp. plain flour

1 cup tomato sauce

16 oz. can okra & tomatoes

½ cup sliced water chestnuts

1 cup diced celery

1/3 cup melted butter

2 tsp. salt

¼ tsp. black pepper

2 tsp. Worcestershire sauce

1 cup water

1 (12oz.) can V-8 juice

8 oz. .can pureed tomatoes

2 lbs. Shrimp

Sauté pepper, onion, celery in butter. Add all other ingredients except shrimp & water chestnuts. Simmer 10-15 minutes. Add Shrimp & water chestnuts. Simmer 10-15 more minutes longer. Serve over Rice.

Submitted by: Brandy Hayes Campbell, daughter

Poultry
of the
Great Pine Level

John Wesley & Katie Lee Henderson

This recipe was my mother Katie Savannah Lee Henderson's. She passed this recipe down verbally to me and my sisters many years ago. Katie was born to Sam and Claudia Lee in Jones Mill/Goodway, Alabama, in 1922. She married John Wesley Henderson of Flomaton, Alabama ,in 1938. They had nine children: Wayne, Geraldine, Catherine, Glenda, Mike, Gale, Kenny, Joyce, and Donald.

This dressing has become a staple at both Hayes and Henderson family reunions. So much so, there was concern that I hadn't made it one year because I used a different pan and my nieces and nephews didn't recognize it! They immediately pulled one of my children aside and asked them where it was. As you can imagine it made my day.

Katie's Cornbread Dressing

1 9 inch pone of cornbread
1 large hen, cut up & boiled for broth
3 sleeves of saltine crackers
6 pieces of light bread
2 cups celery, chopped
2 cups onion, chopped
6 eggs, boiled & chopped
Salt
Pepper
Sage
White pepper

Take Hen out of broth to cool. Take a 12 x 16 pan, crumble cornbread, crackers and light bread. Sauté onions and celery in a little broth. Add to bread mixture. I begin to add salt, pepper, sage, and white pepper to mixture to taste, and then add celery and onion, gradually adding broth until I get the desired consistency. Our family does not like our dressing dry, so don't be afraid to add broth. We also add more crackers or light bread if it tastes too much like cornbread. Add chopped eggs and hen (we put the white meat in). Bake at 375-400 degrees until light brown on top and bubbly on sides.
Note: If hen broth is not rich enough, you can add a stick of butter or can of cream of chicken soup.

Submitted by: Glenda Henderson Hayes, daughter

Cecilia Barnes Hayes

When I first got married, I had no earthly idea how to make chicken and dumplings, but Robert and both loved them so I was determined to learn. I got a recipe, and well, I could never get the dumplings right. I must have thrown out a dozen or more pots of dumplings. They were either too thick, or they would fall apart.

We were living in the white brick house over on Arthur Ave., and our neighbor was Ms. Ruby Coffey. So I just asked her one day how she made them and what awful luck I was having. That is when she told me that the key to perfect dumplings was to mix your flour with ice water. Ever since then, my dumplings have been perfect. This is my signature dish at family reunions and church dinners. I cook them in my big cast iron pot, and I never have to worry about left overs, because there are never any left!

My youngest daughter Kacie has asked me to teach her how to make this recipe during summer break, so that she can carry on the tradition.

Cecilia's Chicken & Dumplings

4 chicken thighs
8 boneless, skinless chicken tenders
Salt to taste
3 cups self rising flour
2 1/4 cups ice water

Boil the chicken in a large pot (I use my cast iron pot) until done. After they cool (I usually let them sit in the refrigerator over night) de bone the
chicken and cut into bite size pieces. Save all the broth that you boiled the chicken in. If its not but about half full in the pot add a little more water.
Mix 3 cups self rising flour with 2 1/4 cups of ice water. Stir until it is the consistency of cookie dough. Roll the flour out with a rolling pin and cut into pieces the size of dumplings. Place on wax paper on a cookie sheet. You will have 5 or 6 stacks. Place in freezer and freeze. Bring broth to hard boil and put frozen dumplings in one at a time. Stir to keep from sticking. After all have cooked for a few minutes, add milk to mixture to make it very soupy. Add black pepper to taste. This makes a very large pot an d could be cut down in amounts to make smaller pot. I sometimes make my dumplings a week or so ahead of time and freeze.

Submitted by: Cecilia Hayes

Ollie Sheffield Smith

This recipe has been used by my family since my great-grandfather fought for the Confederacy in the Civil War. Chickens were generally saved for their egg laying and eaten only on special occasions or when they were no longer egg producers.

Granny's Chicken and Dumplings

1 freshly killed and dressed farm-fed hen
3/4 cup warm water
5 cups of plain flour
2/3 tsp. baking powder
3 Tbsp. lard/shortening
Salt and freshly ground pepper to taste
1/2 tsp. yellow food coloring
6 cups water

Place hen in large Dutch oven; barely cover with water. Add salt and pepper to taste. Bring to boil. Lower temperature and continue to cook covered, until tender. Remove skin and debone hen and set aside. Sift flour, salt, and baking powder together into mixing bowl. Make well in center; cut in lard, add 3/4 cup of water; mix well. Knead several times until dough becomes hard. Divide dough in half. Sprinkle flour on clean table. Roll out each half thin; cut in to strips about 1 inch by 2 inches. Bring the chicken broth to a boil. Add yellow food coloring. Drop strips of dough into boiling chicken broth, one at a time. Simmer for 20 minutes or until tender. Add deboned chicken and continue to cook on low for 3 minutes. Add water if needed.

Submitted by: Louise Smith Gandy

Vassie Cauley Cannon

My mother Vassie Cauley Cannon was born in Tennville, Alabama on December 22, 1916. She and her family lived in several different towns in Alabama and Florida until moving to Jay around 1930. Shortly after moving to Jay, she met Mr. Andrew C. Cannon, who operated Cannon's Rolling Store for Cannon's General Merchandise Co. They were married on November 30, 1935. This marriage was blessed with a daughter Billie Faye (married to Max Ray Smith) and a son John "Johnny" H. Cannon who was killed in Vietnam at the age of 25.

Mother was known for her chicken and dumplings. We had them at least once a week at home. It was the Cannon Family's favorite food. Mother's family and my father's family would both request she bring her chicken and dumplings to all the reunions.

Vassie Cauley Cannon's Chicken & Dumplings

1 hen or fryer
Water (1 cup)
Salt & pepper to taste
Plain flour (2 cups)

Mother didn't have a recipe. She would fill a large pot with salty water and put the hen or fryer on to boil. She had a big red enamel bowl that was filled with plain flour. She would make a well in the center and put water and salt in the well. She would work the flour into the water with her hand until it made a stiff dough. She would then pinch off part of the dough, and on a floured countertop, she would roll out the dough real thin. It was cut down and across to make squares. She dropped the squares into the boiling broth, one at a time. She did this until all the dough was used. The dumplings were cooked until done and then sprinkled with black pepper to taste.

Submitted by: Billie Faye Cannon Smith, daughter

Billie Faye's Cashew Chicken

Max Ray & Billie Faye Smith

6-8 skinless, boneless chicken breasts	Lettuce
3 cups chicken broth	Green onions
1 bullion cube- chicken	Cashews
Cornstarch	Flour
Rice	Salt & pepper

Cut chicken up in to small chunks. Soak in salt water or milk while preparing other ingredients. Clean and chop green onion. Clean and tear lettuce in to pieces. Remove chicken from water/milk. Salt, pepper and flour. Fry in oil until light brown, while frying chicken combine broth, bullion, soy sauce & cornstarch. Bring to boil and simmer until thickened. Put rice on to cook.

In casserole dish, layer lettuce on bottom. Cover with chicken chunks. Sprinkle the chopped onion over the chicken, then add the cashews. Pour the sauce over the layered ingredients. Serve over rice.

Egg a'la Golden Rod

Donnie Ruth Bragg

Donnie Ruth Bragg, was married to Jack Bragg, and was mother of
Cindy Bragg Baggett and Scot Bragg.
Mom would make this meal on Sunday nights for a quick dish.

4 boiled eggs	2 Tbsp. flour
4 Tbsp. butter	3 cups milk
Salt & Pepper, to taste	Bread for toast

Boil eggs, Melt butter in a sauce pan. Add 2 Tbsp. of self-rising flour
and gradually add milk to thicken for gravy. Add whites of boiled eggs
to milk gravy. Toast bread, pour milk gravy over toast, sprinkle with
egg yolks, and enjoy!

Submitted by: Cindy Bragg Baggett, daughter

Mozell's Cornbread Dressing

Mozell Smith Roberts (1917-2009)

Cornbread:

3 cups white self-rising cornmeal
1/2 cup self rising flour
3/4 cup buttermilk

2 eggs
1/2 cup water
2 Tbsp. bacon drippings

Mix ingredients and pour into well-greased hot frying pan. Bake at
400-450 degrees for approximately 25-30 minutes or until golden
brown.

Cornbread Dressing:

1 boiled chicken and broth

2 quarts cornbread crumbs

8-10 slices of light bread, toasted and crumbled

4 eggs

1 cup of diced celery

1 cup of diced onion

1/2 cup of diced bell pepper

1/2 can evaporated milk

1 cube of butter

Sauté celery, onion, & bell pepper in butter. Mix all ingredients together in large pan that has been sprayed with Pam. Mix in enough broth until mixture is soupy. Salt and pepper to taste. Remove chicken from bones and place meat on top of mixture. Bake at 350 degrees for approximately 1 hour, until brown on top.

Submitted by: Becky Jones, daughter

Rachel's Chicken Casserole

3 cups diced cooked chicken

1 can cream of celery soup

1 cup light mayonnaise

1 cup shredded cheese

2 tsp. chopped onion

2 cups toasted almonds

½ cup sour cream

2 Tbsp. lemon juice

Mix all ingredients together. Place in 9x13 casserole dish.
Melt stick of butter, crush one tube of Ritz crackers. Mix crackers with melted butter and spread over top.
Bake at 350 degrees for 30 minutes.

Submitted by: Rachel Hendricks

Cakes & Cookies
of the
Great Pine Level

Louise "Mama" Hudgens

Louise "Mama" Hudgens was the mother of the Reverend Sam
Hudgens and the grandmother of Miriam Hudgens Ingram.

Mama Hudgens' Lane Cake

Cake:
1 cup butter
2 cups sugar
3 1/4 cups flour

Filling:
1/2 cup butter
1 cup sugar
8 egg yolks
1 cup raisins
3 tsp. baking powder
1 cup milk
8 egg whites, beaten
1 Tbsp. vanilla
1 cup of nut meats, chopped
1 cup coconut
1 tsp. vanilla
1 wineglass of brandy, if desired

Cake: (Makes two 10 inch layers or 4 small layers). Cream butter and sugar together until light. Sift dry ingredients together four times. Add milk to creamed mixture, alternating with flour. Add vanilla to egg whites and fold into mixture. Bake at 350 degrees for 40- 50 minutes or until cake springs to touch.

Filling: Cream butter and sugar together. Add egg yolks and cook in a double boiler, stirring constantly until smooth and thick. Remove from fire. Add raisins, nut meats, coconut, vanilla, and brandy to mixture while it is still hot.

Submitted by: Miriam Ingram, granddaughter

Desmond & Vera Boutwell

This is a cake I remember my Grandmother Vera Campbell Boutwell
making often. It reminds me of her because she loved her "Coca-Cola's"
in the little glass bottles. She was the daughter of Hugh Palmar
Campbell and Ida Dell Diamond. Vera was married to Desmond
Boutwell and they had three children: Donald, Roger & Deborah.

Coca-Cola Cake

1 cup butter
1/4 cup cocoa
1 cup coca-cola
2 cups flour
2 cups sugar
1 tsp. baking soda
1/2 cup buttermilk
2 eggs, beaten
1 tsp. vanilla
1 1/2 cup miniature marshmallows

Frosting:
1/2 cup butter
1/4 cup cocoa
1 box confectioners sugar
6 Tbsp. Coca-Cola
1 cup nuts
1 cup marshmallows
1 tsp. vanilla

Cake: Bring butter, cocoa ,& Coca-Cola to a boil. Add flour, sugar, and baking soda. Mix gently. Stir in buttermilk, eggs, vanilla, and marshmallows. Pour into a greased and floured 13 x9 pan. Bake at 350 degrees for 30-35 minutes.

Frosting: Bring butter, cocoa ,& Coca-Cola to a boil. Add marshmallows, stirring until dissolved. Beat in sugar and vanilla. Stir in nuts and spread over cake.

Submitted by: Tami Boutwell Brown, granddaughter

C.E. & Lela Jane Hayes family

I finally retrieved my antique cookbook from the bookcase in the garage and looked for Grandma's recipes. I found two of her cake recipes and I am sending this pound cake recipe because it is the one she baked most often.

In this picture you will see my grandparents C.E. and Lela Jane with their 8 of 9 children; Mary Frances, Era Dean, Donald, Rubye, Robert, Jesse, Ralph, Fletcher, and David Troy Woodfin (grandson).

Grandma Hayes' Lemon Pound Cake

2 cups plain flour
1 3/4 cups of sugar
2 sticks of oleo
1/2 teaspoon of salt
5 eggs
Lemon Flavoring (to taste)

Combine all ingredients in mixing bowl. Beat 12 minutes at medium speed. Bake 1 1/2 hours at 300 degrees. Do not preheat oven.

Submitted By: Elizabeth "Liz" Woodfin Ewing, granddaughter

Cream Cheese pound cake

2 sticks oleo margin or butter
1/4 cup crisco
2 3/4 cups sugar
7 eggs
(1) 8 oz cream philidelphia soft cheese
3 cups plain flour
1/4 teaspoon soda
flavoring
Cream sugar & butter well
add cream cheese
add one egg at a time beat well add flour
Cook 325 degs % 1 hour 20 minuttes

Hazel Irene Jackson Godwin

Hazel Irene Jackson Godwin was a life long resident of Jay and a member of Cora Baptist Church. She was born July 16,1915, and passed on March 29, 2003. She was married to the late Oree Godwin. Her children , Wayne, Earl (deceased), Theron, and Brenda still live in the Jay area. Most of her grandchildren and great-grandchildren live in the surrounding communities as well. Grannie was known for her Southern hospitality and cooking, especially using vegetables or other ingredients that she and her children grew on the farm.

Grannie's cream cheese pound cake was found tucked away in some old books. It was written on the back of a copy of her church's financial statement.

Hazel Godwin's Cream Cheese Pound Cake

2 sticks of oleo or butter
2 3/4 cups sugar
8 oz. cream cheese, softened
1/2 tsp. soda
1/4 cup shortening
7 eggs
3 cups plain flour
flavoring

Cream sugar and butter well. Add cream cheese. Add one egg at a time, beat well. Add flour. Cook at 325 degrees for 1 hour 20 minutes.

Submitted by: Vicki Gandy Baggett, granddaughter

Katie & Thomas Hall

This recipe is in memory of our grandparents, Thomas and Katie Hall.
They lived on what is now Mart Jernigan Road in the Mount Carmel
community. My grandfather was in the horseshoeing business as well as
farming for many years. This recipe was passed down to their daughter,
Eunice Hall Jordan, who lived in Flomaton. It was later handed down
to her daughters and daughter-in-law: Valera Lowery, Juanita Owen &
Vicky Jordan.

Katie Kessiah Hall's Pound Cake

1 cup- shortening, packed
1 1/2 cups sugar
1/2 cup of evaporated (pet) milk
1tsp of lemon flavoring
2 cups plain flour
5 large eggs or 6 small eggs
1/2 tsp. salt
1 tsp. vanilla flavoring

Cream sugar and shortening, add eggs one at a time, beat well in between each egg. Add vanilla and lemon flavoring. Add flour gradually and milk a small amount at a time. Bake to begin at 300 degrees for 30 minutes, then 350 degrees for 30 minutes.

Submitted by: Valera Lowery, Juanita Owen, T.C. & Vicky Jordan

Leon & Flora Shell

Jessie Dunn Shell made this cake weekly and had this recipe passed
down to her from generations passed. Jessie passed it on to her daughter
-in-law Flora Hendricks Shell, who remembers making this
cake often. Jessie Shell and her husband Leroy Jessie Shell were both
Primitive Baptists, followed their belief of continuing to use and pass
on their expertise and knowledge.

Mama Shell's Buttermilk Cake

1 1/3 cup shortening

1/2 cup butter & 1/2 cup of margarine

2 1/2 cups sugar

3 cups plain flour

1/3 cup buttermilk

6 eggs

1/6 tsp. soda

1 tsp. vanilla

Cream shortening and sugar together. Then add eggs one at a time, until blended. Mix soda in flour. Add alternating milk and flour until all are mixed. Add vanilla. Pour into large tube pan and bake at 325 degrees for 1 hour 45 minutes. Gets better with age.

Submitted by: Flora Hendricks Shell, daughter–in-law

Mamie Idella Hendricks

Mamie Idella Hendricks, with her husband Hubert, pulled up stakes in Allgood, Alabama, in the fall of 1927 and moved south, settling on a farm in the Mt Carmel Community. There they raised corn, peanuts, cotton, soybeans and most importantly, ten children-- five boys and five girls.

With so many mouths to feed, much of Mamie's time was spent in the kitchen/ her children remember the fried chicken and banana pudding, which were a Sunday dinner staple. A special memory of her family is the holiday meals, featuring a beautifully roasted turkey with her best ever cornbread dressing.

Her kitchen was always filled with aromas of familiar foods made with ingredients like "sweet milk" & "oleo" and her recipe measurements were often gauged with terms such as a "pinch of salt" a "scant" tsp. of soda or a "right smart of" sugar. No matter what the recipe involved each dish was nothing more than a labor of love.

Mamie Hendricks' Fresh Apple Cake

3 cups raw apples, chopped
1 1/2 cup all veg. cooking oil
2 cups sugar
3 eggs
1 1/2 cups flour
1 tsp. salt
1 tsp. soda
2 tsp. baking powder
1 tsp. vanilla

Sugar Glaze:
1 1/2 cups powdered sugar, sifted
1 cup pecans, chopped
3 Tbsp. water
2 tsp. vanilla

Peel & core apples, chop & set aside. Pour vegetable oil into large bowl. Add sugar and eggs, beat well. Sift flour with salt, soda ,and baking powder. Gradually add flour to creamed mixture. Add vanilla. Gently fold in apples. Grease a 10" tube pan and line with waxed paper. Pour batter in and bake at 350 degrees for 1 hour or until done. When cake is cool remove from pan and drizzle with Sugar Glaze.

Sugar Glaze:
Sift sugar into a bowl. Moisten with water and add vanilla. Drizzle over cake. If too stiff add a little more water. Decorate top of cake with pecans.

Submitted by: Rachel & Mary Evelyn Hendricks, daughters-in-law

Mary Ethel "Marie" Auvil McCaskill

Mary Ethel "Marie" Auvil McCaskill (1896-1983) was married to Benjamin Montgomery McCaskill. They had seven children: Benjamin Montgomery, Jr., James Mack, and Jack Auvil (identical twins), Harry, Mary Elinor, Joy, and Van. She and her husband, also known as "Gum," raised their family on the five-generation family farm in the Ebenezer community. After her husband died, Marie spent the latter part of her life living in Pensacola with her oldest daughter, but she loved returning to Jay, visiting her family and long-time friends. Her favorite pastime was baking, bream fishing, growing lovely roses, and huge, beautiful ferns.

Marie's Pound Cake

1 cup butter
3 cups plain flour, sifted
6 eggs
1/6 tsp. soda
1/3 cup shortening
2 1/2 cup sugar
1/3 cup buttermilk
1 tsp. vanilla

Cream butter, shortening, & sugar. Add eggs, beating after each. Add vanilla. Sift dry ingredients together; add alternately with buttermilk. Place mixture in a greased and floured tube pan. Bake 1 hour & 15 minutes at 350 degrees.

Submitted by: Cynthia McCaskill Brock, granddaughter

Todd & Pearl Floyd

Todd & Pearl Floyd were born & raised in the Jay area. They had nine children: Lois, Helen, June, Hazel, J.T. Dorothy, G.W., Curt, & Carl. Both are now gone on, but their memories live on, especially through some of Pearl's recipes.

A tribute, by JoAnn Carnley Williamson

Being the oldest grandchild, I have a lot of beautiful memories, and I am always telling stories to my brothers, sisters, grandchildren and friends about my grandparents. I think back how they worked from day-light to dark to make a living and provide for their children, and they never complained. There was not big equipment; most of the work was doneby hand or mule and plow.

There was always work to be done, but there were good times, too. There was always "food" on the table and a little wooden "safe" with goodies in it, such as teacakes on a plate. They looked just like little biscuits, and they were the best! Anything my grandparents did was with love and it showed with a smile when we would come visiting.

Pearl Floyd's Tea cakes

2 eggs
2 cups brown sugar
1 cup shortening
1 cup buttermilk
1 tsp. soda
4 cups flour, sifted
1/4 tsp. nutmeg
1/2 cup nuts, chopped (optional)

Cream shortening and sugar. Add eggs one at a time, beating well after each egg. Add a dab of the sifted dry ingredients and beat well. Then add a dab of the milk and beat well. Repeat this 'til the dry ingredients and milk are all gone. Add nuts. Drop by tablespoonful onto a greased cookie sheet. Bake at 375 for 12-15 minutes. (you can also sprinkle sugar on each teacake after it has been taken out of the oven).

Submitted by: Alicia Floyd, Dorothy Lee & Jo Ann Carnley

Ruby Kent

Our mother, Ruby Kent, was an excellent cook. She truly enjoyed
spending time in her kitchen, preparing wonderful meals. Delicious
taste and attractive presentation were important to her; calorie counts,
cholesterol, and obesity never crossed her mind. She liked to see her
family and guests (the family pets) eat heartily and enjoy their
food. Praise & appreciation for her efforts were expected. Daddy set the
example for us children, thanking her after every meal. Occasionally,
one of us five kids (usually Jeanette or Lonnie) would balk at eating
certain foods, usually vegetables. Mother could understand why one
might not like broccoli, eggplant, or rutabaga the way "some people"
fixed it. But the way she fixed it? Incomprehensible why anyone
wouldn't eat and enjoy it! Rex, Bobby, and I would eat everything set
before us. We didn't want to annoy Mama. We loved our Mother and
appreciated her in lots of ways, not just for being a great cook. She had
a quirky sense of humor we all enjoyed.

Ruby Kent's Chocolate Pound Cake

1/2 lb. butter

1/2 cup shortening

3 cups sugar

5 eggs

3 cups All purpose flour

4 Tbsp. Cocoa

1/2 tsp. baking powder

1/2 tsp. salt

1 cup milk

1 Tbsp. vanilla

Frosting:

2 cups sugar

2 Tbsp. cocoa

1 stick of butter

1- 5 oz. can evaporated milk

Cream together (5 minutes) butter and shortening, add sugar and eggs. Sift dry ingredients together and add, alternately with milk and vanilla, to creamed mixture. Pour into greased and floured 9 or 10 inch round tube pan. Bake at 325 degrees for 1 hour and 20 minutes.

Submitted by: Kathryn Kent Miller, daughter

Apricot Nectar Cake

Cake:
1 pkg. yellow cake mix
3/4 cup canned apricot nectar
4 large eggs

Glaze:
3/4 cup confectioner's sugar, sifted
3oz pkg lemon gelatin
3/4 cup vegetable oil
Grated zest of 1 lemon
2 Tbsp. fresh lemon juice
4 Tbsp. of canned apricot nectar

Place rack in center of oven and preheat it to 325 degrees. Lightly mist a 12 cup Bundt pan with vegetable oil spray, then dust with flour. Shake out flour and set pan aside.
Place the yellow cake mix, gelatin, apricot nectar, oil, lemon zest, & eggs in a large mixing bowl. Blend with electric mixer on low speed for 1 minute. Stop the machine and scrape down the sides of the bowl with a rubber spatula. Increase the mixer speed to medium & beat for 2-3 minutes or more, scraping the sides again if needed. The batter should look thick and smooth. Pour the batter into the prepared pan and place in the oven. Bake the cake until light brown and springs back when lightly pressed with your finger (40-42 minutes). Remove from oven and place on wire rack to cool for 10 minutes.

Prepare the Glaze: Combine all ingredients in a small sauce pan and heat over medium-low heat, stirring until sugar has dissolved (3-4 minutes).
Run a long sharp knife around the edge of the cake and invert it onto a serving platter. While the cake is still warm, poke holes in the top with a tooth pick or a long wooden skewer. Spoon glaze onto the cake so that it seeps down in to the holes. Let cake cool before slicing.
Store cake covered in plastic wrap or under a glass cake dome at room temperature for up to one week. Or freeze it wrapped in aluminum foil for up to 6 months.

Submitted by: Joanne (Whaley) Lowery

Era Dean Hayes Woodfin's Apple Cake

4 cups of diced apples
3 cups of plain flour
1 1/2 cups of sugar
1/2 cup of brown sugar, firmly packed
1 cup pecans, chopped
1 tsp. cinnamon
1/2 tsp. cloves
1 tsp. soda
1 1/2 tsp. salt
1/2 tsp. nutmeg
2 eggs
3/4 cup cooking oil
1 tsp. vanilla

Mix all dry ingredients together. Add oil and eggs to mixture. Bake 70 minutes at 350 degrees in a 10 inch tube pan or two 8 or 9 inch cake pans. Cake will be firm when done.

Cream Cheese Frosting:

2 - 3 oz. pkgs of cream cheese
2 Tbsp. of milk or cream
5 Cups of confectioner's sugar, sifted
1 1/2 tsp. vanilla
Soften Cream Cheese- blend in milk/cream, gradually stirring in sugar. Add vanilla, blend well. Frost top and sides.

Submitted by: Elizabeth "Liz" Woodfin Ewing, daughter

Mama's Lemon Cake

In loving memory of Ethel Vinson. My grandmother had nine children and then I came along and was raised along with her last three, we never got sweets very often. Thanksgiving and Christmas to be exact. She had several cakes she baked during those holidays, and I chose my favorite one to share.

Cake:
3 eggs
2 cups sugar
1 cup butter
1 1/4 cups milk
3 tsp. baking powder
Flour

Filling:
5 lemons (juiced & grated)
2 cups sugar

Cake: Cream butter and sugar. Add one egg at a time. Add milk and baking powder and mix well. Add enough flour to make the right thickness for batter (about 2 1/2 cups). Cook in thin layers. Granny always used a flat iron skillet.

Filling: Mix well and let set for a while before cooking. Cook until sugar melts. Take off heat.
This is more of a glaze you pour it onto the layers individually and let it drain the sides and then add another layer until you've finished with the layers and then drizzle all over the top of the cake.

Submitted by: Wendy Diamond Booker, granddaughter

Mamie's Chocolate Icing

Her grandchildren remember the cakes with perfect chocolate icing prepared routinely for them to enjoy.

Most of Mamie's recipes were in her head. She rarely used her
cookbook. (We regret not having written down her method of making
cornbread dressing and fried apple tarts) Her kitchen was always filled
with aromas of familiar foods made with ingredients like "sweet milk"
and "oleo" and her recipe measurements were often gauged with terms
such as a "pinch of salt", a "scant" tsp. of soda ,or a "right smart of"
sugar. No matter what the recipe involved each dish was nothing more
than a labor of love.

2 cups sugar
3 Tbsp. cocoa
1/4 cup Karo syrup
1/2 cup milk
1 tsp. salt
1 tsp. vanilla
1 stick of margarine

Mix together and boil rapidly for 1 minute. Remove from heat and beat
until loses gloss and is thick enough to spread. This icing hardens very
quickly so don't wait too long to put on the cake. This recipe is also
delicious poured over graham crackers

Submitted by: Rachel & Mary Evelyn Hendricks

Nell's Special Red Velvet Cake

This cake is different from the standard Red Velvet Cake with cream cheese frosting. It was always our family's favorite dessert during the Christmas holidays. Since our mother died, my sister Rosemary has perfected our mother's recipe and keeps the tradition of serving it on Christmas Day.

3/4 cup shortening
1 3/4 cup sugar
3 eggs
2 Tbsp. vanilla
3 cups of cake flour
3 Tbsp. cocoa
1 1/2 cups buttermilk
1 1/2 tsp. vinegar
1/4 tsp. salt
1 1/2 Tbsp. soda
3 oz. red food coloring

Icing:
4 1/2 Tbsp. flour
1 1/2 cup sweetened milk
1 1/2 cup sugar
Dash of salt
1 1/2 cup shortening
3 Tbsp. vanilla

To make cake layers, cream shortening & sugar together. Add eggs. Beat until light and fluffy. Add vanilla. Mix dry ingredients and add to mixture, alternating with buttermilk. Add red food coloring & vinegar. Bake at 350 degrees for approximately 30 minutes. (Makes 3 layers)

To make icing, combine flour, salt, & milk. Cook slowly until thick on the stove top. Set aside and cool completely. Mix shortening, sugar, and vanilla. Add to cooked mixture and whip with a mixer. Ice cake layers. (garnish with chopped pecans if desired)

Submitted by: Cynthia McCaskill Brock, daughter

Ann Boutwell's Sour Cream Pound Cake

My mama is Ann Fore Boutwell. This is her recipe that I request every year for my birthday, and she obliges me.

3 sticks or 1 cup of butter
3 cups sugar
6 eggs
3 cups all-purpose flour, sifted
1/4 tsp. soda
pinch of salt
1 tsp. vanilla
8 oz. sour cream

Beat sugar and butter together, add eggs, beat well after each egg. Add all dry ingredients, then sour cream, and vanilla.
Bake 1 hour 15 minutes at 325 degrees in Bundt pan.

Submitted by: Kelly Boutwell Whitman, daughter

Cassie Lowry's Lemon Supreme Cake

1 cake mix (yellow or lemon supreme)
3/4 cup Mazola oil (corn oil)

Glaze:
1 cup confectioners sugar
1 cup apricot nectar
4 eggs
1/2 cup sugar
juice of 3 lemons

Mix together. Grease pan (Tube or Bundt). Pour in pan. Bake in a pre-heated oven at 350 degrees for one hour or when cake springs back when touched.
Glaze: Mix and pour over cake.

Submitted by: Sandra Holt, daughter

Cassie Lowry's Pound Cake

1/2 lb. shortening
6 eggs
2 cups plain flour
1 2/3 cup sugar
1 tsp. vanilla

Cream sugar and shortening. Add eggs one at a time, beating after each. Add flour a little at a time. Stir in vanilla. Pour in to tube pan that has been covered with wax paper and greased. Bake at 300 degrees for 1 hour or when cake springs back when touched.

Submitted by: Sandra Holt, daughter

Sour Cream Nut Cake

I found this recipe in a very old church recipe book. I have made it many times, and it's just delicious.

3 cups flour
3 cups sugar
2 sticks (1/2 lb.) butter
1 tsp. vanilla
6 eggs, break 1 at a time in batter
1/2 pint sour cream
2 1/2 cups of nuts

Mix ingredients together. Bake about 1 1/2 hours at 300 degrees. Don't walk in the kitchen, because the cake falls easily.

Submitted by: Betty Hendricks Salter

Emma's Karo Butter Frosting

Emma Hendricks

I found this recipe for cake frosting in my box of recipes that which my husband's mother gave to me. Ms. Emma Hendricks.

½ cup butter
¼ tsp. salt
½ cup cocoa
3 ½ cups XXXX sugar (confectioner's)

1/3 cup Karo syrup
½ tsp. vanilla
2 Tbsp. milk

Mix together well and top cake.

Submitted by: Virginia Golden Hendricks

Crews Reunion Cake

Crews Family Reunion- Circa 1955

This cake recipe came into the Crews Family when Annie Ruth Holland married Alvin Crews. I grew up eating this cake at every Crews Reunion.

Preparation: Oil two (2) 8" griddles. Preheat oven to 350 degrees. Mix frosting for cake and cook frosting on low heat while preparing and cooking the cake layers.

Frosting for Cake:

3/4 cup sweet milk

2 cups sugar

1/2 cup butter

1 1/2 tsp. vanilla

Cake

(White Part):

3 eggs

1 cup buttermilk

1/2 cup butter & 1/2 cup lard	1 cup sugar
2 1/2 cups flour	1 tsp. salt
1 1/2 tsp. soda (set aside)	

(Dark Part):

| 1 cup cocoa | 3/4 cup buttermilk |
| 1 cup sugar | 1 1/2 tsp. vanilla |

In two small bowls, mix white & dark parts separately. Then combine mixes in one large bowl and mix well.

Put a thin layer (pancake style) of mix in griddles for 15 minutes. Turn out on towels, put cake layer in plate upside down (the frosting soaks in better with layers upside down). Put about 1/3 cup frosting on each layer. Repeat, (should wind up with 6-8 layers.) Top layer should be topside up.

Submitted by: Dorothy Crews Penton, niece

Jeanette's Plucking Cake

Clifton & Jeanette Lowry

Jeanette Salter Lowry grew up in Chumuckla, Florida. She was the ninth of ten children. She was an avid basketball player and graduated from Chumuckla School. She married her high school sweetheart, Clifton R. Lowry, on May 24, 1952. They grew up together, learning how to hunt, fish, grow their own food and cook it. Out of their love came three children: Gail Deese, Nancy Daugett, & Clifton Lowry, Jr. Over the years, Mama shaped and molded her recipes to fit her family. She was and is still known as a great cook.

We have many memories of growing up around our table. Everyone was always welcome and always had plenty to eat. Our parents taught us to always love each other, share with everyone ,and respect one another. We treasure each memory we make and each recipe we try. We hope you will enjoy them, too.

Submitted by: Gail Deese, daughter

Plucking Cake

3 cans biscuits

2 Tbsp. Cinnamon

1/2-1 cup pecans

1 cup sugar

1 stick of margarine

Mix sugar and cinnamon. Cut biscuits into 4 pieces and roll in sugar and cinnamon mixture. Grease a Bundt pan. Layer first can of coated biscuits in pan. sprinkle more sugar and cinnamon over layer and then nuts. Layer 2 & 3 repeat. Melt margarine and pour over cake. Bake at 350 degrees for 30 minutes. Turn out of pan immediately.

Loma Lee's Buttermilk Pound Cake

Loma Lee Nowling & Family

1 cup shortening

3 1/2 cups all purpose flour

1 stick butter

1/4 tsp. baking soda

2 1/2 cups sugar

1 Tbsp. boiling water

1 cup buttermilk

4 eggs

1 1/2 tsp. vanilla

dash of salt

Beat shortening & butter until creamy. Add sugar, continue beating until very creamy. Add eggs one at a time. Sift flour with baking soda & salt. Add alternately with buttermilk, beating well between additions. Add vanilla. Add boiling water & beat well. Pour in to greased Bundt pan. Bake approximately 1 hour at 300 degrees.

Submitted by: Joy Nowling Moore, granddaughter

Mamie Lou's Pound & Black Cakes

Mamie Lou Eddins Nowling

Mamie Lou Eddins moved to Jay in 1915 at the age of three, from Pineapple, Alabama. She later met the dashing young Arthur Nowling at the Crossroads School where they both attended. They were married at Jay Methodist Church in October of 1933. They purchased a piece of paradise from Arthur's Uncle Pete Nowling and began farming row crops, chickens, and two little girls.

Mamie Lou Nowling was an accomplished quilter, excellent cook, a loving wife, and mother. She also delivered several babies in the community.

Mamie Lou's Pound Cake

6 eggs
3 cups sifted cake flour
2 1/2 cups sugar
5 Tbsp. Milk
1 cup shortening

Cream shortening and sugar. Add eggs, one at a time. Add flour a little at
a time with milk. Beat good. Pour in greased & floured tube pan. Bake at 300 degrees.

Black Cake

1 cup shortening
2 Tbsp. Saver's cake spice
3 eggs
3 1/2 cups all purpose flour
2 cups sugar
1 cup buttermilk
2 cups raisins
2 cups pecans

Mix shortening & sugar until creamy. Add eggs one at a time. Mix flour and spices together & add to mixture a little at a time with milk. Stir in pecans and raisins. Bake in 10" pan for 1 hour 30 minutes at 300 degrees.

Mary Alvia Burgess' Pound Cake

Mary Aliva Browning & T.G. Burgess Family

Mary Alvia Browning was born September 17, 18186 to James
Madison Browning Jr. & Mary Jane Smith Browning. In Clay county,
AL. in 1904 "Alvie" married Truman Granville Burgess. In 1930, they
moved their large family to the Jay area. Mrs. Alvie was a loving
mother and devoted pastor's wife. She was a caring woman with a
generous spirit and a whole bunch of children to feed. A single cake
didn't go far between 14 children, a husband and a constant flow of
visitors and dinner guests. She leaned more to the "dab of this" ,and "a
little of that" than to a recipe. Therefore this recipe may not be exact,
but it ought to be pretty close.

1 lb. butter	dash of salt
4 cups plain flour	1 tsp. vanilla
8 eggs- separated	1 cup milk
5 Tbsp. orange or lemon Juice	3 cups sugar
2 tsp. baking powder	

Cream butter& sugar, then add egg yolks. Beat well. Add juice, vanilla,
and milk. Add flour, baking soda, and salt. Beat egg whites until very
stiff, then fold into mixture. Bake at 300 degrees for 1 hour or so.

Submitted by: Joy Nowling Moore, great-granddaughter

Nellie's Marble Pound Cake

Nellie Smith May (1913-1996) *married to Ted May*

1 cup shortening
3 cups of sugar
6 eggs
3 cups sifted cake flour
1/2 tsp. salt
1/4 tsp. soda
1 cup buttermilk
1 tsp. vanilla
1 5.5oz can chocolate syrup

Cream shortening & sugar; add eggs, one at a time, beating well after each. Sift together flour, salt and soda. Add to creamed mixture, alternately with buttermilk. (begin and end with milk). Add vanilla. Pour half of batter into a greased and floured 10" tube pan. Add chocolate syrup to remaining batter. Pour chocolate batter over top of batter in pan and gently fold or stick spatula down in batter to get marble effect. Bake at 350 degrees for 1 hour and 1o minutes.

Submitted by: Becky Jones, niece

Robert's T- cakes

Robert Hayes, David Troy Woodfin & Ralph Hayes

I remember as a child coming home from school in the afternoon and Mama would have cookies similar to these ready for us with a big glass of milk. Every kid in Jay knew they could come over to Ms. Hayes' and there would be cookies for snacks.

2 cups of shortening (butter flavor)
3 eggs
2 cups sugar
1 tsp. vanilla
4 cups self-rising flour

Cream shortening in a large bowl, Add sugar, mixing well. Add eggs and vanilla, mix well. Stir in flour. Turn dough out onto a lightly floured surface. Knead gently. Roll dough our in to 1/4 inch thickness. Cut with a 2 inch biscuit cutter. Place on a lightly greased cookie sheet and bake at 350 degrees for 10 minutes or until lightly browned. Coat with granulated sugar to taste.

Submitted by: Robert Hayes

Scarlett & Meme's Chocolate Cake

Scarlett Moore & "Meme" Betty Sue Dyess Nowling

1/2 cup sugar
1/2 cup flour, self rising
1/2 stick melted butter
1/2 cup buttermilk
3 Tbsp. cocoa powder
1 egg
1 tsp. vanilla flavoring

Beat sugar & egg, add butter and mix well. Add flour and cocoa, then buttermilk & vanilla. Grease and flour 5"or 6" pan. Bake at 350 for 10-15 minutes. Cool and frost with vanilla or chocolate frosting. Add lots and lots of sprinkles.

Cassie's Orange Slice Fruit Cake

Cassie Windham

1 cup butter	3 ½ cup plain or cake flour
2 cups Sugar	1 lb. chopped Dates
4 eggs	1 lb. Orange Slices Gum Candy
1 tsp. soda	1 can flake coconut
½ cup buttermilk	2 cups pecans

Cream butter, sugar, add milk & eggs. Gradually add flour. Leave a little bit to roll dates in. Chop dates and orange slices. Add rest of ingredients and mix well. Cook at 300 degrees for 1 hour or until done. While still hot, mix 2 cups of powdered sugar and 1 cup of orange juice. Pour over cake and let cool.

Pauline Brook's Layered Fruitcake

Estelle Brooks Laney

Pauline Brooks was my mother. This is her Layered Fruitcake recipe she made.

¾ cup shortening
2 cups sugar
4 eggs
1 cup sweet milk
4 cups self rising flour
   Sifted with,
1 tsp. allspice
1 Tbsp. cloves
1Tbsp cinnamon

1 box white raisins
1 jar fig preserves
1 box of dates
½ lb. candied cherries
2 pieces candied pineapple
2 pieces orange peel
2 pieces of lemon peel
1 cup nuts

Chop all fruits and nuts, then roll all the fruit and nuts in the flour mixes with spices. Cream shortening & sugar, add eggs, mix well. Add fruit with milk a little at a time. Bake in layers at 325 - 350 degrees for 40 minutes.
Filling:

Juice of 4 oranges
1 large can crushed pineapple
1 cup chopped nuts

Grated rind of 1 orange
2 cups sugar
Butter size of an egg

Cook until thick. Let Cool, then spread between layers.

Submitted by: Estelle Brooks Laney

Betty Simmons' Pound Cake

Betty Simmons

This pound cake is one the best cake's ever made. Betty often makes it for dinners at her church and has shared it with many family and friends in the community.

Betty was born in Orlando, Florida on June 12, 1931. She grew up in the Chumuckla community and has lived in Santa Rosa County ever since.

She worked at Judy Bond in Brewton, Alabama for 19 years, and worked at Providence Manufacturing in Flomaton, Alabama for 8 years. Her mother was Edna Nettles Ard and her father was Sam Ard. Betty had two daughters, and she is the wife of W.L. Simmons.

Beat well together:
2 cups sugar   1 cup oil
6 eggs

Add 2 cups of Swan's Down Cake Flour (be sure to use this brand)
¼ tsp. salt
1tsp vanilla (or any other flavoring you may desire)

Beat well and pour into greased Bundt cake pan. Bake at 350 degrees until done.

Leslie Ham Stewart's Ice Box Fruit Cake

1 cup pecans
1 bag marshmallows (lg)
1 can sweetened condensed milk
1 box seedless raisins
1 box graham crackers
1 box coconut

Mix ingredients together in large bowl. Crumble crackers, add milk, mix well and press into pan and fridge to chill.

Submitted by: Marian Stewart Griffin, granddaughter

Lela Jane's Ice Box Fruit Cake

Lela Jane Owens Hayes & Columbus Euenn Hayes

Lela and C.E. were married Valentine's Day 1925 . She was born in Haleyville, Alabama. She, C.E. and their growing family moved here from Etheridge, TN around 1938 after her father and mother A.F. & Pansy Jane Meeks Owens sent for them. She reared 9 children: Era Dean, Jesse Owens, Mary Frances, Donald Oscar, Rubye Elizabeth, Euenn Fletcher, William Ralph, Robert Lee & Roger Philip.
This is one of her recipes that was her children's favorite. To this day, it is a must for family gatherings and holidays.

1 box Vanilla Wafers, crushed
1 can condensed milk
1 cup raisins
1 cup shredded sweetened coconut
1 cup pecans, chopped

Combine all ingredients and mix well. pour mixture in to greased loaf pan. Chill and serve. Freezes beautifully.

Cassie Morris Lowry

Cassie Morris Lowry, wife of Hubert H. Lowry raised 14 children.
She was born and lived in Jay all of her life. She was our mother and
on of the world's best cooks. Our table seated 12 easily and was always full of a variety of meats, vegetables, and desserts. She cooked
enough that each of us would have something that we liked. When
visitors were present near meal time they were always invited to eat
with us. Usually they were happy to do so. Every day when we would
come home from school she always had something delicious waiting
for us. About the only thing she used recipes for were the desserts.
Every Christmas the Icebox Fruitcake was made in three or four varie-
ties in order to please each of us . She died in 1980 at the age of 66.

Cassie Lowry's Ice box Fruitcake

1/2 box graham crackers
1 can condensed milk
1 stick of margarine, melted
1/2 bag vanilla wafers
1/2 bag of chocolate chips
1 cup pecans, crushed

Crush together graham crackers and vanilla wafers. Add condensed milk. Add all other ingredients. Mix well and make in to rolls. Roll in tinfoil and refrigerate. Other variations she made were: instead of chocolate chips add cherries and coconut or raisins in the place of chocolate chips.

Submitted By: Sandra Lowey Holt & Martha Boutwell, daughters

Betty Sue's Mississippi Mud Cake

Betty Sue Dyess Nowling

3 cups sugar	2 tsp. baking soda
1 cup butter- melted	½ tsp. salt
1 tsp. vanilla	1 ¼ cup cocoa
3 ¾ cups all purpose flour	1 ½ cups buttermilk
1 ½ cups boiling water	

Preheat oven to 350 degrees. Grease 2 10" pans. In large bowl, beat sugar & butter. Add eggs and vanilla. In med. Bowl, combine flour, soda, salt & cocoa. Gradually add to sugar/butter mixture, Alternate with buttermilk. Slowly add boiling water. Beat until just combined. Spoon into pans and back 28-34 minutes. Cool in pans for 10 minutes. Remove and cool completely.

Mississippi Mud Filling:

8 oz. whipped topping	7oz Marshmallow Cream
4 oz. cream cheese	1 cup toasted pecans, chopped

Combine above ingredients till smooth. Stir in Pecans. Cover and chill one hour. Layer between cakes.

Chocolate Cream Cheese Frosting:

1 cup soft Butter	8 oz. cream cheese
9.7 oz. bittersweet chocolate melted and cooled	1 tsp. vanilla
6 cups confectioner's sugar	

Beat butter and cream cheese until creamy. Add melted chocolate, gradually add confectioner's sugar. Add vanilla.

Spread Frosting evenly on top and sides. Garnish bottom edge of cake with mini marshmallows. Sprinkle marshmallows and pecans on top of cake and drizzle with chocolate syrup.

Jay Cafeteria "Boiled Chocolate Cookies"

In the early 1950's, students of Jay School ate a hot lunch each day in the "lunchroom". This little white frame building fed many, many students great meals. The cooks always cared that each student had enough to eat and often prepared items which students liked the best. The food items and ingredients were delivered from USDA and were of fine quality from U.S. farms. Such things as pure butter, powdered whole milk, flour and oatmeal were among the items used to make good, wholesome dishes. One of the items made were the "Boiled Chocolate cookies". That might not sound appetizing, but those little cookies were the favorite of almost every single student as well as the teachers. This recipe has been altered to make 24 large cookies, but the one in the school kitchen, their recipe made over a hundred.

2 cups sugar
1/2 cup milk
1 stick of butter
4 Tbsp. cocoa
2 1/2 cups quick cooking oatmeal
1/4 cup nuts, chopped
2 tsp. vanilla
1/2 cup peanut butter (optional)

Cook sugar, milk, butter, and cocoa. Bring to rolling boil and cook for 1 1/2 minutes. Remove from heat and add oats, nuts, peanut butter and vanilla. Mix until well blended. Spoon onto wax paper.

Submitted by: Dorothy Diamond

Pies, Desserts, and Candy
of the
Great Pine Level

Cassie Lowry's Lemon Creme Pie

1 can condensed milk
6 oz. frozen lemonade concentrate
4.5 oz. whipped topping
2 graham cracker crusts

Mix the three ingredients together and pour in to crusts. Let cool in at least 3 hours in the refrigerator.

Submitted by: Sandra Holt, daughter

Mary's Fresh Strawberry Pie

1 cup of sugar
3 Tbsp. cornstarch
1 prebaked pie crust
2 cups Fresh Strawberries. sliced
3 Tbsp. strawberry Jell-O (dry)
1 cup water
Whipped topping

Mix sugar and cornstarch together. Add water. Cook over low heat until thick. Remove from heat and add Jell-O. Wash and drain strawberries. Slice strawberries and place in baked pie crust. Pour cooled mixture over the strawberries . Let cool. Serve with Whipped topping.

Submitted by: Natasha Boutwell Walters, granddaughter

Mama's Peanut Candy

I am submitting this recipe in honor of my grandmother Ethel Vinson. You had to be special for her to make this candy, but if your were lucky she would make it and the aroma of the nuts parching was out of this world!

1/2 bag of Co-op Peanuts
2/3 Jar (1/2 gallon) Blackburn Syrup
1/2 stick Margarine

Parch peanuts and grind them up until a very fine texture. Boil the syrup and margarine in a cast iron skillet for about 2 minutes on high. Turn off and add peanuts. Mix well and pour into an oblong pan that has been sprayed or oiled.

Submitted by: Wendy Diamond Booker

Dorothy Arnette Diamond

Dorothy Arnette Diamond was born September 17, 1937, in Pensacola, Florida. She married Marshall Diamond, and they have four children. Dorothy loves cooking for her family so much. Almost every child and grandchild has had a birthday cake at her house every year and often she makes this 4 layer dessert for family dinners. She can double it for a large crowd and it is always a great success. Family diners have always been the high-light of her life, and she will use any excuse she can think of to get everyone together.

It would please her very much if she knew that each of her children learned how to make this dessert and would make it a tradition at their homes.

4-Layer Chocolate Dessert

First Layer:
1 cup plain flour
1 1/2 sticks of butter
1 cup nuts, chopped

Second Layer:
8 oz. cream cheese
1 1/2 cups confectioner's sugar
1 sm. carton Cool Whip

Third Layer:
2 boxes of instant pudding mix (chocolate)
3 1/2 cups milk

Fourth Layer:
1 lrg. carton of Cool Whip
Grated Chocolate, nuts or peppermint candy, etc.

First layer: Melt Butter; stir in flour and nuts. Press into pan. Bake at 350 degrees for 10 minutes.

Second layer: Mix well and spread over cooled crust

Third layer: Combine pudding and milk. Beat for 1 minute (will be soupy) pour onto second layer. Let it set in the refrigerator until firm.

Fourth layer: Top with cool whip. Garnish with grated chocolate, nuts, etc.

Jimmy Floyd Owens

As far as I know this pie is originally from Edna Owens Fulmer from the branch of the family tree of Albert Lafayette Owens in Lauderdale County, Alabama. The adaptation is mine for chopping some of the apples, too, and adding more cinnamon. the original instructions were sparse too, so I completed them so anyone can bake the pie without prior baking knowledge. I've been making this recipe for about 15 years and is a family favorite by request or demand.

I got this recipe by way of my father Jimmy Floyd Owens because of his love of family history. This is picture of him after he left Jay and went into the Army. Jimmy is my father and was Arthur & Pearl Owens' son. I am one of the Great Granddaughters of Fletcher and Pansy Jane Owens.

Owens' Fresh Apple Pie

3/4 cup sugar

1 egg, beaten

1 1/3 cups peeled & shredded apples (4-5 granny smith)

2 pie crusts

1/4 cup brown sugar

3/4 tsp. of cinnamon (I use 1)

3/4 tsp. cornstarch or flour

3/4 stick of butter, sliced.

Combine all ingredients, except butter. Put into unbaked pie crust, top with butter. Place top crust on to pie; crimp and trim edges. Cut 4-8 small slits in top crust to vent. Bake at 400 degrees for 15 minutes; then 30 minutes at 325 degrees. Let cool and enjoy!

If desired before baking, brush top with milk for browning crust, brush with egg white for shiny, browned crust. (I use milk)

Submitted by: Teresa Owens Casey, daughter

Letha Myers

Letha Myers was married to Curt Myers. She was a native of Chumuckla, Florida. She had four children, six grandchildren, eight great grandchildren and four great-great grandchildren. She inspired many and was loved by all. She won first place at the Jay Peanut Festival with this delicious pie in 1981. It was also a big hit at the church cake walks.

We try and try to make one just like hers but none can make like our Granny Myers.

We love and miss her very much!

Peanut Butter Pie

1 cup powdered sugar
1/2 cup peanut butter
3/4 cup granulated sugar
1/2 tsp. vanilla
1/4 cup cornstarch
1/4 tsp. salt
2 cups milk
3 eggs, separated
1 Tbsp. margarine

Blend together powdered sugar, and peanut butter with pastry blender or 2 knives. Will be the consistency of a crumbly mixture. Bring granulated sugar, cornstarch, salt and milk to scalding point. Separate 3 eggs. Beat yolks together. Then add eggs to milk mixture. Cook until thick, stirring to keep mixture smooth. Remove from heat. Add 1/2 teaspoon of vanilla and 1 Tbsp. of margarine. Put 2/3 of the peanut butter mixture on bottom of crust. Pour custard in shell. Beat egg whites with 3 Tbsp. sugar and a pinch of cream of tartar. Put on custard. Add remainder of peanut butter mixture to meringue. Bake in over at 350 degrees until meringue is done.

Submitted by: Lisa Diamond, granddaughter

Marshall Diamond's Chocolate Ice Cream

Most of Marshall's family and friends know that ice-cream is his favorite food. Whenever he and I, have company he always wants to make ice-cream. Marshall considers serving home-made ice-cream a privilege and a treat. he created this recipe for himself and has made it many times over the years. The first time he made it he used an old hand crank type freezer and as the ice cream hardened, one of the children would help him hold it down while he turned the crank. Many happy times were had around that old freezer and there was nothing better to eat on a hot summer day.

2 cans sweetened condensed milk
1/4 cup Hershey's Chocolate syrup
1/2 cup granulated sugar
1 quart Chocolate milk
1 med. carton Cool whip, thawed

Mix sweetened condensed milk, and sugar with mixer until well incorporated. Add Hershey's syrup. Beat well. Add Chocolate Milk slowly while beating. Mix well. Fold in Cool Whip.
Pour into electric freezer and freeze according to freezer directions.

Submitted by: Dorothy Diamond, wife

Mary Boutwell's Pecan Pie

Mary Dent & Carson Boutwell were married in 1938. Their family consisted of four hungry little boys to be fed through the 40's and 50's. Mary was blessed with a talent of reproducing delicious meals from the most basic ingredients: homegrown vegetables, meats and cornbread. Meats were often fried chicken, pork chops. or fish. She had a reputation in the Pine Level community as "one who could whip up a cake or pie on a moments notice". They were always good, as there were never any sweets left on the table.

1/2 cup sugar
1 cup White Karo Syrup
3 Tbsp. butter
1 cup pecans, chopped
1 tsp. vanilla
3 eggs

Mix sugar and syrup; bring to a boil. Add butter. Pour the hot mixture over beaten eggs. Add pecans and pour in to unbaked pie crust. Bake at 300 degrees for 35-40 minutes. Makes 2 small pies or 1 large pie.
Hint: Bake pie on a preheated cookie sheet and the crust on the bottom will be brown.

Submitted by: Martha Boutwell, daughter-in-law

Annie Ruth's Washday Candy

Sarah Annie Ruth Byrd Crews

Sarah Annie Ruth Byrd Crews ,wife of Julian I. Crews. Mother of Emery, Dorothy Nell Crews Penton, Roy Martin Crews and Betty Ruth Crews Simmons.

This is one of my favorite memories of my maternal grandmother. She would cook up a batch of candy and the pulling and stretching would keep me busy while she got the wash and other chores done.

2 c cane syrup	Pinch of baking soda
1/4 c water	1/2 stick of oleo

Cook syrup and water on low heat in an iron skillet, stirring constantly, until it reaches hard boiled stage.

Add the soda and turn out onto well buttered waxed paper. Butter your hands and as soon as possible, start to pull pieces of the candy. Keep stretching and pulling until color is light blonde. Twist and lay in a well buttered plate.

Submitted by Paula Lewis, granddaughter

Cora Burkhead's Peanut Brittle

1 cup sugar
1/3 cup Karo or light corn syrup
1 1/2 cups raw peanuts
1 tsp. soda

Cook slowly until all peanuts are almost done. Remove from heat, add soda. stir as little as possible. Pour on to a buttered surface spreading it out. When cool break into pieces.

Submitted by: Betty Scott Burkhead, daughter-in-law

Charline's Coconut Pie

Charline Hood Warrick, Laura Hood Kalata, Judy & Kayla Flowers

Growing up, if grandma knew I was coming for a visit she always made this for me. When I got older and attempted myself, well you know the outcome. It was not only not as good as grandma's but not fit to eat! Back to grandma I went to figure out why. Well as you will see in the recipe it calls for 3 tablespoons of flour. Well she uses one of the serving spoon sizes for her tablespoon. So I wasn't adding enough flour! But then she also started adding a little cornstarch which helped. It takes patience and you must stir it every minute while on the stove, but if you do you will have a wonderful pie! I hope to pass along these little "tidbits" to my children and hope you enjoy this recipe too.

Pie:

1 baked pie shell

1 cup sugar	3 cups milk
3 Tbsp. flour	1 tsp. vanilla
1 tsp. cornstarch	1/2 tsp. salt
3 egg yolks	1 cup coconut

Mix sugar, salt, flour and cornstarch. Add egg yolks with 1 cup milk and blend well, add the other 2 cups of milk.. Cook over medium heat, stirring constantly until thick. Remove from heat and add coconut and vanilla. Pour in baked pie shell and top with meringue. Sprinkle with coconut and put in oven to brown meringue.

Meringue:

Beat 3 egg whites till stiff peaks form. Add 1/2 cup sugar, 1 tsp. at a time.

Submitted by: Judy Baker Flowers, granddaughter

Mary Boutwell's Apple Tarts

Carson & Mary Boutwell

Mary Dent Boutwell was my paternal grandmother. I was taught how to make these tarts by her before I started Kindergarten

1 box Betty Crocker Pie Crust Mix   2 cups sugar
1 bag of dried apples

Place apples in boiler with just enough water to cover. Soak for 30 minutes. Cook apples on low for 20 minutes. Remove from heat and add 2 cups of sugar. Mash apples up with sugar until all large pieces are gone. Place in fridge and cool for 2 hours or until cool. Mix pie crust mix as package directs. Roll out small ball of dough on floured surface as thin as possible to form oval shape about 8x6. Place 2 teaspoons of the apple mixture in the center of the bottom half. Fold top half of dough over to cover the apples to form a half circle shape. Put on a baking sheet and bake at 425 degrees for about 10 minutes or until golden brown.

Submitted by: Natasha Boutwell Walters, granddaughter

Ralph's Favorite Strawberry Pie

William Ralph Hayes, Sr.

Wm .Ralph Hayes Sr. was born October 2, 1941 to C.E. & Lela Jane Hayes. He was a life long resident of Jay and married Glenda Henderson of Flomaton on July 6, 1968. He passed on January 25, 2009.

He and my mom stumbled upon this recipe on one of their spring drives looking for fresh strawberries. They decided to try this pie after finishing shopping at Burris' Farmers Market & Daddy just loved it, and asked for the recipe. He got it and we renamed it "Ralph's favorite strawberry pie"

1 cup Confectioner's sugar
8 oz. whipped topping
2 cups, fresh strawberries, chopped

8oz. cream cheese, softened
1 graham cracker crust

Combine sugar & cream cheese. Add whipped topping, fold in strawberries. Place in pie crust & chill.

Submitted by: Jane Hayes, daughter

Ruth Hudgens' Divinity & Mud Hens

Reverend Sam and Ruth Hudgens

Ruth Hudgens is the mother of Miriam Ingram. She was the wife of Reverend Sam Hudgens, former pastor at Jay United Methodist Church. She had four children, Betty Nichols of Mobile, the late Sam Ellison Hudgens, Jr., Miriam Ingram of Jay, and Louisa Watson of Plantersville, Alabama.

She and brother Sam were in the ministry for many years.

Sea Foam or Divinity

3 cups of white sugar
3/4 cup of white corn syrup
3/4 cup hot water
3 egg whites
vanilla
nuts

Cook sugar, syrup and water until it spins a thread, or it forms a hard ball in cold water. Pour it in slowly to stiffly beaten egg whites, add the vanilla and nuts but not too soon.
Stir until its ready to drop by teaspoonful on a buttered platter or wax paper. Food coloring in small amounts maybe added for a variety as well as different flavorings.

Mud Hens

1 stick oleo
1 cup sugar (brown or white)
1 1/2 cups sifted plain flour
1 tsp. baking powder
1 pinch of salt
1 Tbsp. vanilla
3 eggs (1 whole, 2 yolks)

Cream butter, sugar, egg yolks and one whole egg. Add flour and vanilla. Spread in square or oblong pan. Sprinkle 1/2 cup of pecans on top of raw batter. Then spread on filling. Beat one egg white with 1 cup of brown sugar. Bake about 30 minutes at 325 degrees.

Submitted by Miriam Hudgens Ingram, daughter

Wayland's Crustless Egg Custard

Wayland Nowling

8 eggs
3 cups milk
1 1/2 sticks butter

3 cups sugar
2/3 cup self rising flour
1 Tbsp. vanilla

Beat sugar & eggs, add flour. Add milk and beat well. Add melted butter & vanilla. Mix. Butter 9 x12 dish. Pour into dish and bake at 350 degrees about 40 minutes.

Submitted by: Joy Nowling Moore, daughter

Bessie's Peanut Brittle

Bessie Morris Edwards

Bessie Edwards was born in Jay, Florida, November 1913. Her parents were William "Bill" Morris & Edna Bass Morris. Bessie was the only daughter of eight children, so she learned to cook and keep house at an early age. Bessie married Elbert Edwards.

One of her favorite recipes was Peanut Brittle. She made it for many family and church gatherings and it was favorite of all ages. Her recipe is fool-proof if you follow the directions carefully.

1 cup of sugar   ½ cup Karo syrup
½ cup water

Cook until mixture "spins a thread" when poured from spoon.

Add 1 cup raw peanuts

Cook to "hard crack". This means the peanuts will begin to make a popping sound. Add 1 tsp. soda, 1 tsp. butter & 1 tsp. vanilla. Stir well & pour on to a greased pan. Stretch the hot mixture with your hands as it cools on the pan. When completely cool, break in to pieces.

Evelyn's Humdingers

Evelyn Westmoreland

1 stick Oleo

¾ cup sugar

8 oz. box dates, chopped fine

1 ½ cup Rice Krispies

1 cup chopped pecans

Melt butter and sugar over low heat and stir constantly. Add the dates and keep cooking over low heat until mixture is gummy. Cook 5-8 minutes longer until dates are all to pieces. Remove from heat and add Rice Krispies and nuts; Mix well, but do not mash. When cool, shape and roll in powdered sugar.

Momma's Chocolate Oatmeal Candy

Louise Jackson

2 cups sugar
¼ cup cocoa
½ cup milk
1 tsp. vanilla

4 Tbsp. Peanut Butter
¼ lb. margarine
3 cups Oatmeal

Mix sugar, cocoa, & milk. Cook 3 minutes. Stir in vanilla, peanut butter, margarine and oatmeal. Drop by spoon on cookie sheet.

Ethel Golden's Egg Custard

Ethel Golden

This recipe was written down on a piece of paper from my mother Ethel Golden. She made lots of these custard's because my daddy, Charlie Lee Golden really liked them!

1 cup sugar	1 tsp. vanilla
1 ½ Tbsp. flour	1 cup milk
1/3 stick of butter	Nutmeg (optional)

With mixer add 1 egg at a time until you put 4 in.

Beat well, put in pie plate. Bake at 300-350 for 40-45 minutes.

Submitted by: Virginia Golden Hendricks, daughter

Virginia's Pear Cobbler

Virginia Golden Hendricks

Virginia Hendricks, daughter of Charlie & Ethel Golden, married to
B.D. Hendricks and have two children; son Richard "Ricky" David
Hendricks, wife Nina. Daughter Vicki Renee Hendricks Laney, hus-
band Timothy "Tim", five grandchildren; Brandt David Hendricks,
Rush Davis Hendricks, Tessa Louise Hendricks, Tanner Brooks Laney
& Todd Golden Laney.

1 qt. of pears in bottom of casserole dish (cut pears small).
Sprinkle ½ cup water over pears. Mix 1 stick butter/oleo, 1 cup self ris-
ing flour, 1 cup of sugar, & 1 tsp. vanilla. Mix & Crumble over pears.
Cook 1 hour at 300 degrees.

Mama 'Call's Buttermilk Pie

Nathia McCall

My grandmother, Nathia McCall, made this pie whenever we were going to visit her. It was my favorite dessert and I always looked forward to arriving at her house for a slice of Buttermilk Pie. We always called her Mama 'Call and she was a very good cook.

Prepare one unbaked 9- inch pie shell. Brush inside of shell with un-beaten egg white so that is will brown on bottom.

Blend together:
¼ cup melted butter   1 ½ cup sugar
1 heaping Tbsp. plain flour

Add & beat together:
2 beaten eggs   ½ tsp. vanilla
¼ tsp. lemon zest   Pinch of salt
1 cup buttermilk (Use whole buttermilk for better taste)

Pour mixture into unbaked pie shell. Sprinkle with nutmeg. Bake at 450 for 10 minutes, reduce oven to 350 and cook until mixture is set.

Submitted by: Jessica McCall Blaize, granddaughter

Nadine's Banana Pudding

Nadine "Granny" McCurdy

This is my favorite recipe because when I worked at Jay High School, I would always make this banana pudding for our homecoming at Mt Carmel UMC. Thad Soloman, Lisa Hayes & Kelly Hayes would always ask me during the week if I was going to make that Banana Pudding for Sunday. And you know, I always did to please them.

3 pkgs. Instant Vanilla pudding
3 cups whole milk
Using mixer blend pudding mix and milk.

Fold in:
8 oz. Sour Cream
1 lg. container whipped topping

Alternate layers of vanilla wafers and sliced bananas and pudding. This recipe calls for 5-8 bananas and large box of vanilla wafers. Makes about 12 servings.

Myra Fore

Myra Fore was my dear mother, she was married to Woodrow Fore, they had 5 children, Ann Boutwell, Carolyn Smith, Patsy Kirkland, Gerald Fore and Emily White. Baking was my mother's specialty. She was known all over Brewton and East Brewton for her cakes and pies. She was busy most holidays baking special order cakes and pies for those lucky enough to get one.

Myra Fore's Coconut Cream Pie

1/2 cup sugar
1/2 cup sweet milk
1/2 tsp. salt
3 eggs, separated
1 9 inch pie crust
1/3 cup flour
1 stick oleo
1/2 tsp. vanilla
1 small can coconut

Mix flour, sugar and salt. Add small amount of milk to form paste. Add beaten egg yolks and beat together. Add remaining milk and oleo. Cook until thick. Add vanilla and coconut. Pour in to pie crust and cover with meringue. Bake at 325 degrees until golden brown.

Submitted by: Ann Boutwell, daughter

Other

of the
Great Pine Level

Floy Mae & Roy Ingram

Floy Mae Ingram was a native of Arkansas. She was married to Roy
Ingram of Jay. She had three children; Thelma Wenning of Gulf
Breeze, Robert Ingram of Jay, and Rema Campbell of Pace. She is
Miriam Hudgens Ingram's mother-in-law. She was a hard worker at
home and helping on the farm. She was a great cook and person.

Floy Mae's Pear Mincemeat Preserves

7 lbs Pears

1 lemon

2 lbs. seedless raisins

6 3/4 cup sugar

1 Tbsp. cloves

1 Tbsp. cinnamon

1 Tbsp. nutmeg

1 Tbsp. allspice

1 Tbsp. ginger

Grind pears, lemon and raisins. Combine remaining ingredients in extra large pan. Add ground fruit and bring to a boil over medium heat. Simmer for 40 minutes. Pack in jars. Process in hot water for 25 minutes.

Submitted by: Miriam Hudgens Ingram, daughter-in-law

This photo was taken in October 1966. It was to be the last official group photo of the complete Leo Miller family. Originally from Enterprise, Alabama, the family has resided in the Wallace area of Santa Rosa county since 1938.

Mama Miller was known as a good cook even before she married at age 16. As the years passed, her cooking skills increase. Her youngest daughter Carolyn Tidwell, used her mother's bread and butter pickles recipe numbers of times and often brought a jar of the tangy, crisp pickles to family gatherings. Several years ago, she shared it with her brother Lomax, who had it in mind to make some pickles like "Mama used to make". Some of his grandchildren recall his first batch well, for he had them do the chopping of all the ingredients. Granddaughter Jillian Miller (Jernigan) even sent a quart of these pickles to some friends in Ireland. These Irish friends had been so impressed by the biscuits she made them while there on a summer mission trip that she decided a jar of "Pa's" pickles, along with the recipe, would constitute a fitting Christmas gift. The pickles also received rave reviews.

The recipe may well have originated with Georgia Miller Martin's mother, or with her mother-in-law. Who knows how many family members have also used it! When Carolyn first shared the recipe with her brother he called it "Carolyn's Pickles." A few batches and many jar's later, it phased into " Pa's Pickles", "Daddy's Pickles" or "Lomax's Pickles"- depending upon one's relationship to the head of the Lomax Miller family.

Lomax's pickles

Slice several onions, jalapeño peppers, on green bell pepper and two large red peppers.
Slice 25-30 cucumbers (or squash, etc.)
Add 1/2 cup of salt

Soak cucumbers in ice water for 3 hours or more, drain off ice water.
Mix equally, 5 cups vinegar with 5 cups of sugar.
Mix together mustard seeds, celery seeds, a tsp. turmeric, and 1/2 tsp. whole cloves.

Bring spices, sugar and vinegar to a boil in a large pot. Add the cucumbers and bring the mixture almost, but not quite to a boil again. Pack the cucumbers into jars, covering with the liquid, and seal.

Submitted by: Gaylier Miller, wife

Pepper Jelly

Minnie Leddon Smith

Pickles, relishes, preserves and jellies considered delicacies, were a must on Grannie's table. She believed that the key to success was to use only the best cider vinegar.

1 1/4 cups of pepper, half sweet & half hot
6 1/2 cups sugar
1 1/2 cups cider vinegar
1 6-7oz Bottle Pectin
3 or 4 drops of red or green food coloring

Combine peppers, sugar and cider vinegar in kettle; bring to boil 2 minutes with full heat. Remove from heat; let stand 5 minutes. Stir in pectin and food coloring; mix well. Pour in to hot sterilized jars; seal. Process in boiling water bath for 10 minutes. Makes 6 1/2 pint jars.

Submitted by: Louise Gandy

Rochelle Walters Arnette's Lime Pickles

Preserving fruits and vegetables was an important task for Rochelle.
She was born in Hacoda, Alabama, in 1913 and grew up in Pensacola,
Florida during the Great Depression. Rochelle learned this recipe for
Lime Pickles from her mother Lila BarkerWalters.

Families always found a way to make use of every fruit and vegetables.
Nothing was thrown away. If it was not eaten by the family, it was fed
to the dogs, cats, chickens or hogs.

Preserving lime pickles was a way to use extra cucumbers from the
garden and were enjoyed all year with dried or canned vegetables and
meats. Lime can be purchased at almost any super market today.

3 cups of lime
2 quarts of water
cucumbers
6 cups sugar
3 cups vinegar
1 large pkg. pickling spices
1 tsp. salt
Green food coloring

3 cups of lime in 2 quarts of water. Cover chopped cucumbers and soak
24 hours.
Drain and wash. Put in clear ice water for 4 hours. Change water every
hour. (adding ice each time). Drain well.
Bring to a boil: sugar, vinegar, pickling spices, salt and food coloring.
Let stand over night. Next day simmer 1 hour and place in jars and seal.

Submitted by: Dorothy Arnette Diamond, daughter

Mary Dent Boutwell's Canning Tomatoes

Pour boiling water over tomatoes until skin slips off. Cover and let tomatoes come to a boil (in own juice). Stir from bottom; when them come to a full boil place in jar with juice on top. Add 1/2 tsp. salt in each pint and seal jars. Cover jars with water and let boil 5 minutes.

Submitted by: Martha Boutwell, daughter-in-law

Ollie Whaley's Strawberry Fig Preserves

6 Cups figs, mashed
4 cups sugar
6oz .pkg. of strawberry Jell-O

Mix together figs, sugar and Jell-O. Let this mixture sit for 40 minutes.
Boil slowly for about 20-30 minutes, stirring constantly.
Pack while hot in to sterilized jars, Seal with canning (rubberized) lids.
4 pints

Submitted by: Joanne (Whaley) Lowery

Quick Strawberry Preserves

3 cups of fresh figs, mashed (approx. 2 lbs.)
1 1/2 cups of sugar
3 oz. pkg of strawberry gelatin
combine figs and sugar in a heavy saucepan; cook over medium heat,
stirring constantly 2 minutes.
Gradually stir in gelatin, and cook over low heat, stirring constantly for
15 minutes.

Spoon preserves in to hot sterilized jars, filling to 1/2 inch from top.
Remove air bubbles; wipe jar rims, cover at once with metal lids and
bands. Process in boiling water bath 5 minutes. Makes 4 1/2 pints

Submitted by: Jane Hayes

Floy Mae's Never – Fail Dill Pickles

Use fresh Dill or recently frozen dill stalks with heads.

Wash cucumbers and pack in sterile jars with Dill heads in top and bottom. For each quart, boil together the following; 1 cup water, 1 cup vinegar,1 Tbsp. salt.

Pour hot liquid over cucumbers. Seal tight. Set jars in canner and cover
with boiling water. Put lid on canner and let set over night until cold.
Remove next day and store. You can use medium or small cucumber or
split large ones to make it fit into jars. For best results, let set for 3
months before using.

Submitted by: Mariam Hudgens Ingram, daughter-in-law

All Healing Black Salve (Skin Cancer Healing Recipe)

Truman Granville Burgess

Truman Granville Burgess (T.G.) was born in Clay county, Alabama on April 21, 1886, to James Joel Burgess & Martha Jane Haynes Burgess. December 11, 1904, he married Mary Alvia Browning. God blessed them with a total of 14 children, my grandmother (Loma Lee Burgess Nowling), being one of them.

In 1930 the Reverend Burgess moved the lot of them to the Jay area. During his life here, he pastored many of the area's churches- including Pine Level, Cora and Calvary. He was a member and past Master of Jay Masonic Lodge #176.

Great-Grandaddy Burgess was also an avid fisherman. This seems to be a strong trait passed down through the generations.
T.G. Burgess died March 24, 1970. He is buried in Cora Cemetery.

All Healing Black Salve

* Passed on to Truman G. Burgess by and older man in his community.

2 oz. Bees Wax
2 oz. Rosin
4 oz. Red Lead
2 Drachms pulverized camphor

Melt Bees Wax and Rosin together. When near boiling point, stir in
Red Lead. When nearly cool, stir in camphor.
To pulverize camphor, pour a little alcohol on it.

Submitted by: Joy Nowling Moore, great granddaughter

Aunt Sallie Soloman's Cocoa Snuff

Sallie Vaughn Soloman

Sallie Vaughn Soloman was an "honorary Aunt" in our community and was a "mail order bride" for Mr. Soloman, a widower with children. She was an old maid schoolteacher from Vaughnville, AL. & arrived by train in Flomaton many years ago to help him raise his children. The Soloman's & their daughter Arissia Soloman Johnson, lived across the field from us, close to Pineview Methodist Church near Hollandtown. Aunt Sallie told us never to dip snuff. but she would show us how to make our own snuff for children. She kept detailed records of everything and gave us empty snuff cans to use.

1 cup sugar   pinch of salt
1/2 cup Hershey's cocoa
Mix good and fill snuff cans.

If we got tired of practice "dipping" then we would make chocolate milk from her recipe!

Submitted by: Joyce Schnoor

Granny Godwin's Cough Medicine

Hazel Irene Jackson Godwin

Boil one lemon slowly for 10 minutes. Get juice out of it. Add 2 Tbsp. of glycerin. Stir Glycerin and juice well. Fill glass with water in which you have the juice. Drink up.

The End

Unlock more "Tastes and Tales of the Great Pine Level" in Volume 2! With more great stories of families from the area, along with pictures and great recipes.

www.jayhistoricalsociety.org

Jay Historical Society
Jay, Florida